™

Star Trek
Toys by Playmates

™

The Unauthorized Handbook & Price Guide

4880 Lower Valley Rd. Atglen, PA 19310 USA

Kelly Hoffman

Disclaimer

Copyright © 2000 by Kelly Hoffman
Library of Congress Catalog Card Number: 00-100877

Designed by Bonnie M. Hensley
Type set in Americana XBd BT/Zapf Humanist BT

ISBN: 0-7643-1127-1
Printed in China
1 2 3 4

Published by Schiffer Publishing Ltd.
4880 Lower Valley Road
Atglen, PA 19310
Phone: (610) 593-1777; Fax: (610) 593-2002
E-mail: Schifferbk@aol.com
Please visit our web site catalog at **www.SCHIFFERBOOKS.COM**

In Europe, Schiffer books are distributed by Bushwood Books
6 Marksbury Avenue Kew Gardens
Surrey TW9 4JF England
Phone: 44 (0)208-392-8585; Fax: 44 (0)208-392-9876
E-mail: Bushwd@aol.com
Free postage in the U.K., Europe; air mail at cost.

This book may be purchased from the publisher.
Include $3.95 for shipping. Please try your bookstore first.
We are always looking for authors to write books on new and related subjects.
If you have an idea for a book please contact us at the address above.
You may write for a free printed catalog.

Dedication

I would like to thank my friends and family for all those years of love and support.

The toy collecting bug bit me way back in 1992. The year Playmates Toys first introduced the Star Trek line of action figures. That first release was only a few figures (the rest would follow). I had no idea what I was getting my family and myself into. Collecting Star Trek toys is a lot like having an addiction.

And if you have traveled to more than two stores in one day looking for that missing toy, chances are you might be addicted to toy collecting too.

Acknowledgments

A very special thank you goes out to Rick at New Force Comics for all the help he has given me and all those other Trek collectors out there. He has been able to bring many of my fellow collectors the much-needed toys for their collections. Check out his website at www.newforcecomics.com.

I also want to thank everyone at 800-trekker.com for all their support while I was working on this book.

A special thanks goes out to Jon (Bart of Borg) Huss for allowing me into his home and his collection to take photos of some of the items my collection is still lacking. Thank you.

I cannot forget a big thank you to all my fellow Playtrekkers. Playtrek is an online group that discusses Playmates Trek toys, hence the name Playtrek. They have been extremely helpful in helping me to locate and obtain many figures for my collection. Special thanks go to Chuck M., Andy N., Taylor K., Liza N., Mel P., Ted N., Dean A., Dale J., Rick W., and the rest of the group. Thanks gang!

Scott at the *Raving Toy Maniac* website for all the news and information on upcoming Trek toys throughout the years. It was through his site that I found Playtrek.

Contents

Foreword

I have been collecting, trading and selling *Star Trek* toys since I was first bitten by that collecting bug in 1992. Soon after buying my first toys I wanted more. Playmates was there to fill that need. Once I was hooked and my collection kept growing, I wanted to know the value of my collection. Doing that soon proved to be a difficult and sometimes confusing task. I would find values listed in different magazines, but would sometimes see the same item listed more than once with a different value and a simple one or two word explanation next to it. How was I, or anyone else for that matter, supposed to know what that meant? There were no photos or explanations as to what they were talking about. I waited many years for someone to write a book or even a simple article in one of the many toy magazines to help explain things. It never came. So now after many years of collecting and research into my own collection I have decided to take the task on myself.

The values placed in this book are based on what many current secondary retailers are asking for the figures plus many other factors, including what I have personally paid and sold figures for. The values are averaged from several of these sources. I have consulted with many top dealers in person, at conventions, and through the internet. The values are only here as a guide and are not intended for commercial use. The values in this book are based on mint in package (MIP) figures, ships and accessories.

I have limited the entries in this book to toys released within the United States. There are a few exceptions to this rule and they will be clearly marked.

For *Star Trek* fans the world over there is a sort of shorthand that has evolved around the series. The original or classic *Star Trek* has become known as the original series or TOS. The first film is often referred to as ST:TMP (Star Trek: The Motion Picture), while the consecutive films that followed are referred to by number (i.e. ST: II, ST: III, ST: IV, ST: V, and ST: VI) along with the title of the film. The later films with the crew of the new *Enterprise* are not usually given numbers, just *titles (Generations, First Contact* or *Insurrection).*

Along with the launch of the Enterprise-D and her new crew came a whole new set of abbreviations. *Star Trek: The Next Generation* is often called Next Gen or simply TNG. The later two series, *Deep Space Nine* and *Voyager,* go by DS9 and VOY respectfully. Throughout this book you will see these abbreviated terms used often.

Just a quick note on how the book is laid out. The book starts out with the 4.5" figures, then proceeds to the other sizes in order, followed by playsets, ships and accessories. Each section is then broken down by assortment number and the year of release. The figures are then listed by the stock number and character name followed by a list of accessories that came with that particular figure.

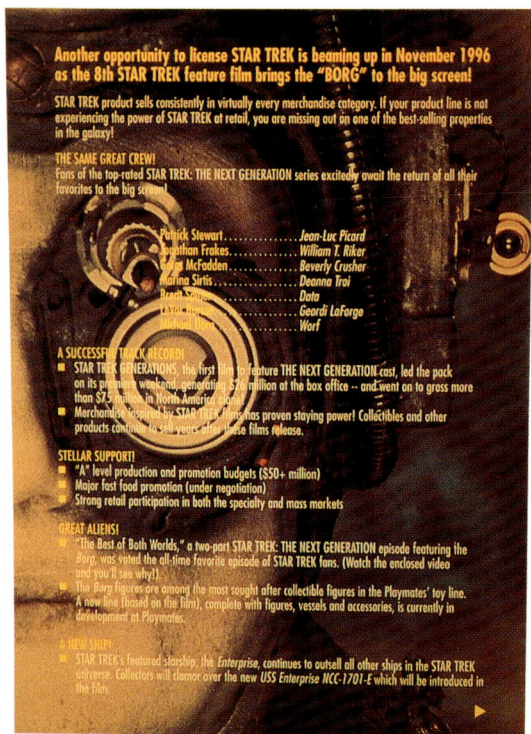

An inside fold from the Trifold Borg showing licensing information for *Star Trek: First Contact.* Photo taken by Dean Andrade. See page 68.

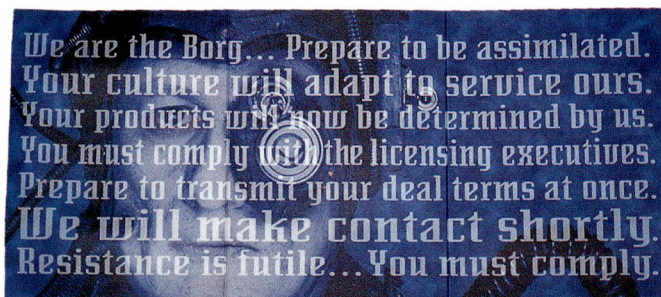

Trifold Borg when completely opened up. *Photo taken by Dean Andrade. See page 68.*

To Boldly Go Where No Action Figure Had Gone Before..

The Playmates Toys Star Trek line started in 1992. Their first assortment of toys (Assort. No. 6010) was from the new television series *Star Trek: The Next Generation*, which began in 1988. This was not the first line of toys for the television series, but it would be the first successful one.

In 1988 the Lewis Galoob toy company was the first to throw their hat into the *Star Trek: The Next Generation* action figure ring. The figures that Galoob produced were in the 3.75" scale, very similar to the hugely successful Kenner *Star Wars* figures. Galoob's ST:TNG figures lacked detail and did not have a great deal of articulation. The first series consisted of six figures. They were Jean-Luc Picard, William Riker, Geordi LaForge, Worf, Tasha Yar, and Data. Due to a production problem four different variations of the Data figure were produced. Data's head had a normal flesh colored face, a spotted face, a blue face, and a very dark colored face. Of those four versions, the blue faced Data is the rarest and therefore the most valuable. Galoob followed their first line with a line of aliens, ships and role-playing accessories. They produced an Antican, Ferengi, Q, and Selay as well as the Galileo Shuttle, a Ferengi fighter, die-cast Enterprise D and Type I Phaser. Lewis Galoob lost their license to make *Star Trek* action figures and so the torch was passed on to Playmates Toys.

Captain Jean-Luc Picard stock no. 6011

Asst. No. 6010 Series 1 *The Next Generation* 1992

Captain Jean-Luc Picard

Stock No. 6011
Type I hand phaser
Tricorder with holster (The holster is actually a part of the figures and comes attached to the leg.)
Personal view screen
PADD (personal access display device is a small hand held computer.)
Starfleet action base
Captain's Log adventure booklet
Value: $25.00

Lt. Worf

Stock No. 6013
Type II hand phaser
Tricorder with holster
Ceremonial Bat'telh sword
Klingon combat blade
Klingon sword
Starfleet action base
Value: $20.00

Lt. Commander Data

Stock No. 6012
Type II hand phaser
Diagnostic testing unit with monitor
Tricorder with holster
Two android access panels one on his right arm and the other on his back.
Starfleet action base
Value: $20.00

Data with access panel on his arm open.

Rear access panel on Data's back.

Commander William Riker

Stock No. 6014
Type II hand phaser
Tricorder with holster
Directional UV source
Away team field kit with detachable analyzer
Starfleet action base
Value: $20.00

Lt. Commander Geordi La Forge

Stock No. 6015
Type II hand phaser
Tricorder with holster
Bio-engineering tools (two different tools)
Dilithium crystals
Away team portable computer gear
V.I.S.O.R. (visual instrument and sensory organ replace-
    ment worn by Geordi LaForge.)
Starfleet action base

There were two different versions of this figure. When it was first released the figure came with a removable V.I.S.O.R. The back of the packaging had a photograph of the figure without the V.I.S.O.R. on. This was later changed and the V.I.S.O.R. was glued to the head of the figure and the image was changed on the back of the package as well.
Value: $20.00; w/removable VISOR: $45.00

Geordi LaForge with the V.I.S.O.R. removed.

Geordi LaForge with V.I.S.O.R.

Back of packaging showing the removable V.I.S.O.R.

Back of packaging showing the V.I.S.O.R. in place.

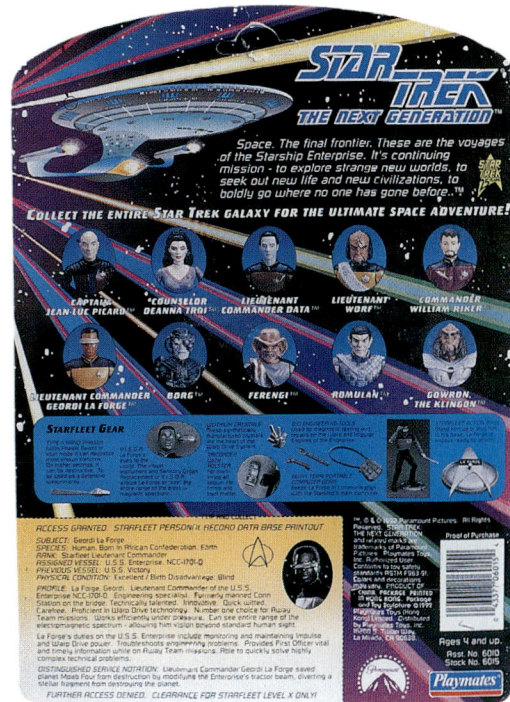

Counselor Deanna Troi (in lavender outfit)
Stock No. 6016
Tricorder
PADD
Portable computer gear
Desktop viewer
Starfleet action base

There are a few different variations of this figure. Perhaps the most notable is in the lower production numbers of this figure, which had a defect that caused the head to fall off. This was later fixed. Figures below 5000 have the flaw. In fact, some have been found in the package with the head loose.
Value: $20.00; numbers under 5000: $35.00

Ferengi
Stock No. 6052
Energy whip
Hand blaster
Ferengi rifle
Dilithium crystals
Ferengi base

There are three different variations of this figure. The most common is the figure with black paint on the boots. Less common is the figure with no black paint on the boots. There is also the reverse Ferengi. The photo of the figure on the back of the package is printed backwards. When compared with the figure, you can see that the Ferengi symbol on the forehead is on the wrong side.
Value: $20.00; no black on boots: $35.00; reverse image: $40.00

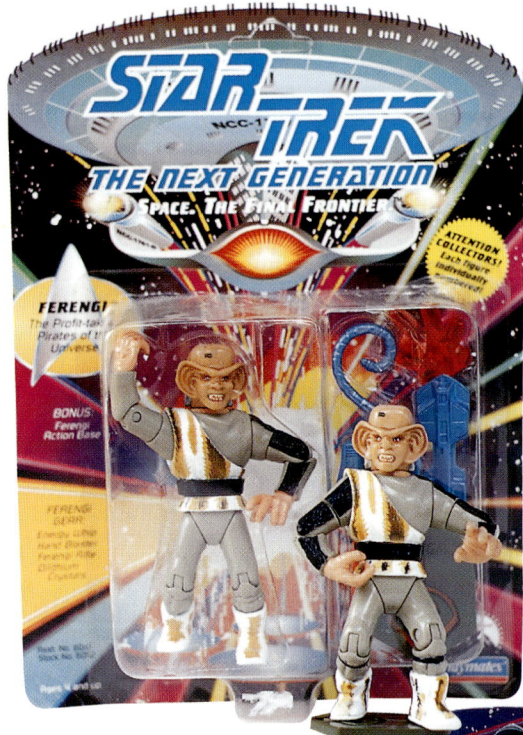

Ferengi without black on boots in package with a Ferengi with black on his boots.

Romulan
Stock No. 6051
Romulan phaser rifle
Romulan disruptor pistol
Romulan PADD
Romulan base
Value: $20.00

Back of packaging showing the reversed image of the Ferengi.

Gowron the Klingon

Stock No. 6053
Ceremonial war club
Klingon disruptor with holster
Targ (a Klingon pet)
Pain stick
Klingon base

The basic figure has gold trim on the shoulder strap, chest plate, belt buckle and legs. There are several variations of this figure. The most valuable of these is the figure lacking any gold trim. However, there are many combinations of paint variations. Some have green paint instead of gold. Some have the trim on the legs painted green with the trim on the torso in gold. There are many other combinations, but the one of value is the figure without any paint on the trim.

Value: $25.00; w/o gold trim: $35.00

Gowron with gold trim on his torso but green trim on his legs.

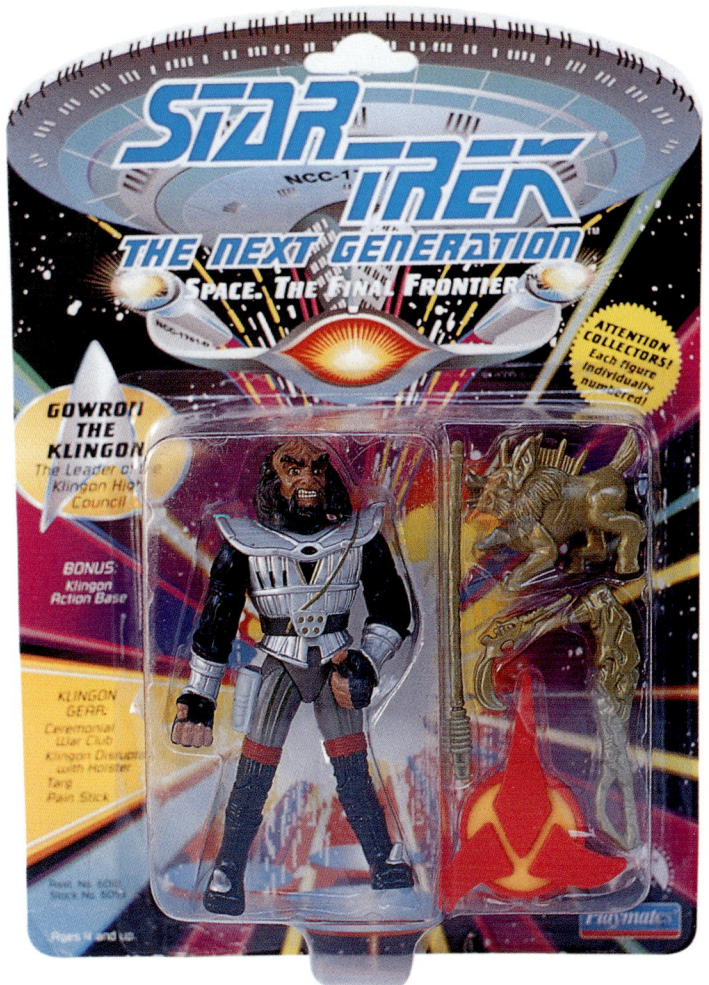

Gowron with gold trim on his outfit.

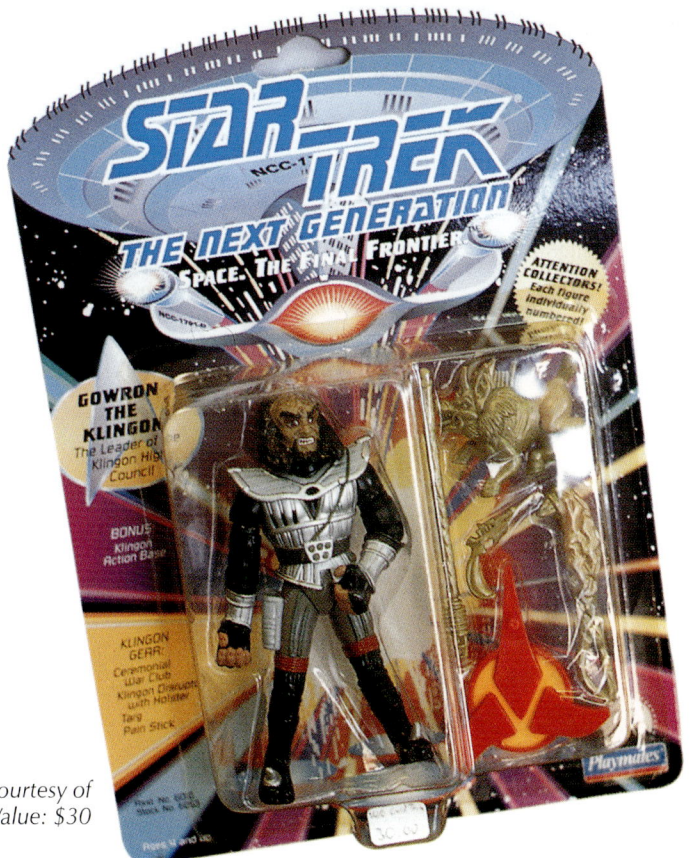

Gowron with all green trim. *Courtesy of Pagoda Comics. Value: $30*

11

Borg

Stock No. 6055

Mechanical manipulation arm

Shield generation coils

Bionic plasmic laser and cutting ray arm

Borg base

As with the Ferengi figure, the Borg figure also has a reverse image on the back of the packaging. Simply compare the photo of the figure against the actual figure and you'll notice the eyepiece is on the wrong side in the photo.

Value: $15.00; reverse: $45.00

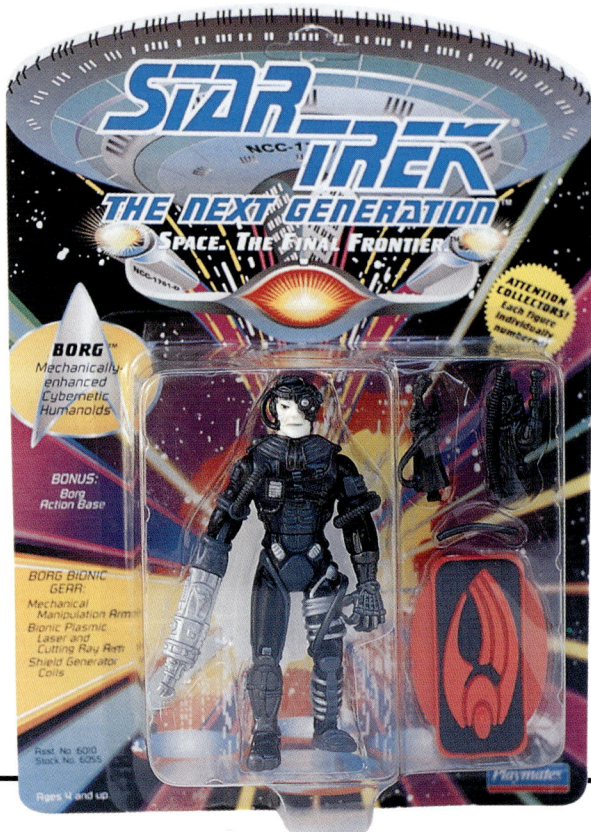

Back of packaging showing the reversed image of the Borg.

Borg stock no. 6055

Assort. No. 6070 *The Next Generation* 1993 Series 2

This series of figures came with a exclusive trading card or space cap (pog) from Skybox. The figure with the pog instead of the card is generally valued higher than the figures with the trading cards.

Dr. Beverly Crusher

Stock No. 6019

Portable medical monitor

Medical tricorder

Portable medical kit

Hypospray

Starfleet action base

Value w/card: $15.00; w/pog: $25.00

Guinan
Stock No. 6020
Drinking glasses
Chess set
Ten-forward tray
Starfleet action base
Value w/card: $15.00; w/pog: $25.00

Lore
Stock No. 6022
Type II hand phaser
Hand held laser
Field kit
Tricorder
Starfleet action base
Value w/card: $10.00;
   w/pog: $15.00

Cadet Wesley Crusher
Stock No. 6021
Type II hand phaser
Portable tractor beam
Tricorder with holster
Starfleet carrying case
Starfleet action base
Value w/card: $15.00; w/pog: $20.00

Locutus (Captain Jean-Luc Picard as Locutus of Borg)
Stock No. 6023
Borg cybernetic hand
Mechanical cybernetic borg manipulator
Shield generator coils
Borg action base
Value w/card: $20.00; w/pog: $30.00

Klingon Warrior Worf
Stock No. 6024
Klingon pain stick
Klingon spiked club
Klingon disruptor
Ceremonial robe
Klingon base
Value w/card: $15.00; w/pog: $25.00

Ambassador Spock
Stock No. 6027
Klingon monitor
Romulan PADD
Romulan phaser rifle
Vulcan book
Vulcan base
Value w/card: $10.00; w/pog: $15.00

Lt. Cmdr. LaForge in Dress Uniform
Stock No. 6026
Type II hand phaser
Desktop viewer
Tricorder
Plaque of medals
Starfleet action base
Value w/card: $10.00; w/pog: $20.00

Admiral McCoy
Stock No. 6028
Medical monitor
Medical tricorder
Portable medical kit
Hyposprayer
Starfleet action base
Value w/card: $10.00

Captain Scott
Stock No. 6029
Dilithium crystals
Engineering monitor
Bio-engineering tools
Multi-range light source
Starfleet action base
Value w/card: $10.00

Mordock the Benzite
Stock No. 6057
Type II hand phaser
Tricorder with holster
Scanner
Monitor
Starfleet action base
Value w/card: $10.00; w/pog: $20.00

Commander Sela
Stock No. 6056
Romulan PADD
Romulan phaser rifle
Romulan knife
Romulan phaser
Romulan base
Value w/card: $10.00; w/pog: $15.00

Q in Starfleet Uniform
Stock No. 6058
Miniature U.S.S. Enterprise
Miniature Earth
Dilithium crystal
Scepter
Starfleet action base
Value w/card: $10.00; w/pog: $20.00

Ambassador K'Ehleyr
Stock No. 6059
Spiked glove
Life support mask
Ceremonial sword
Klingon base
Value w/card: $15.00; w/pog: $20.00

Dathon
Stock No. 6060
Dagger
Log book
Flaming branch
Tamarian knife
Tamarian base
This figure was not released in the United States with a pog. The U.S. release was only with the trading card.
Value w/card: $20.00; Australian release w/pog: $400.00

Vorgon
Stock No. 6061
Tox Uthat artifact
Dilithium crystal
Hex
Vorgon scanner
Vorgon base
Value w/card: $15.00; w/pog: $55.00

Captain Jean-Luc Picard in first season uniform
Stock No. 6071
Type I hand phaser
Tricorder with holster
Personal view screen
PADD
Starfleet action base
Value w/card: $10.00; w/pog: $20.00

Lieutenant Commander Data in first season uniform
Stock No. 6072
Type II hand phaser
Diagnostic testing unit with monitor
Tricorder with holster
Android access panel
Starfleet action base
Value w/card: $15.00; w/pog: $20.00

Commander William Riker in first season uniform
Stock No. 6074
Type II hand phaser
Tricorder with holster
Directional UV source
Field kit with detachable analyzer
Starfleet action base

This figure reused the arms and legs of the first figure. Where the first series figure had tears in his uniform, so does the second series Riker. Only in the second series, the tears in the arms and legs were painted over.
Value w/card: $15.00; w/pog: $20.00

Lieutenant (JG) Worf in first season (red) uniform
Stock No. 6073
Type II hand phaser
Tricorder with holster
Ceremonial Bat'telh sword
Klingon combat blade and sword
Starfleet action base
Value w/card: $15.00; w/pog: $25.00

Side view of Riker showing tears in sleeve and pants leg visible through the paint.

Lieutenant (JG) Geordi LaForge in first season (red) uniform
Stock No. 6075
Type II hand phaser
Tricorder with holster
Bio-engineering tools
Away team portable computer gear
V.I.S.O.R.
Starfleet action base
Value w/card: $15.00

Borg with chrome arm
Stock No. 6077
Multifunctional rotation arm
Hydraulic mechanical ram arm
Shield generator coils
Borg base
Value w/card: $15.00; w/pog: $30.00

Counselor Deanna Troi 2nd Season Uniform (red out-fit)
Stock No. 6076
PADD
Portable computer gear
Desktop viewer
Tricorder
Value w/card: $15.00; w/pog: $25.00

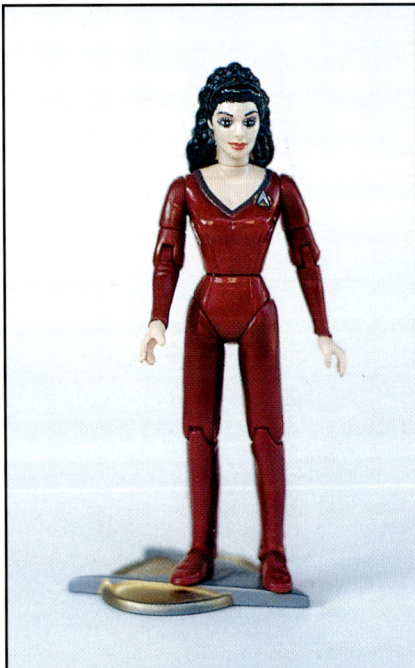

Assort. No. 6200 *Star Trek: Deep Space Nine* 1993

The figures in this series came with an exclusive Skybox card.

Commander Benjamin Sisko
Stock No. 6201
Type II hand phaser
PADD
DS9 monitor
Bajoran Orb case
Starfleet base
Value: $10.00

Odo
Stock No. 6202
Bajoran PADD
Bajoran tricorder
Bucket sleeping chamber
DS9 monitor
Bajoran base
Value: $10.00

Chief Miles O'Brien
Stock No. 6204
Type II hand phaser
Engineering kit
Laser drill
Fire extinguisher
Starfleet base
Value: $10.00

Quark
Stock No. 6203
Ferengi head cane
Reptilian pet
Gold press latinum bars
Exotic beverage bottle
Ferengi hand blaster
Ferengi base
Value: $15.00

Lieutenant Jadzia Dax
Stock No. 6205
Tricorder
Trill
Bio sample collector
Field hypospray
Portable computer gear
Starfleet base
Value: $20.00

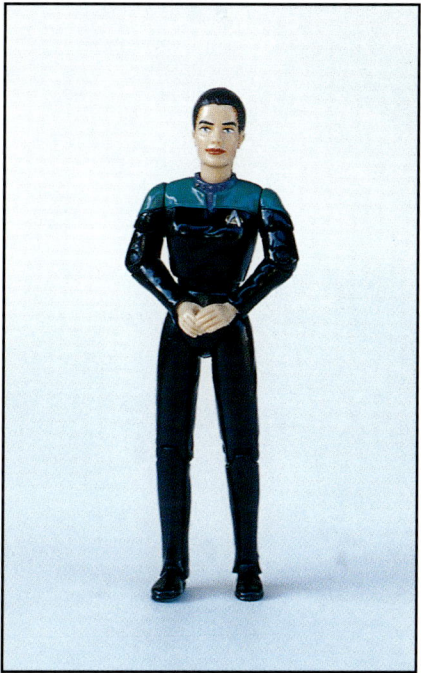

Major Kira Nerys
Stock No. 6206
Bajoran pistol
Bajoran tricorder
Duffle bag
Bajoran PADD
Bajoran base
Value: $15.00

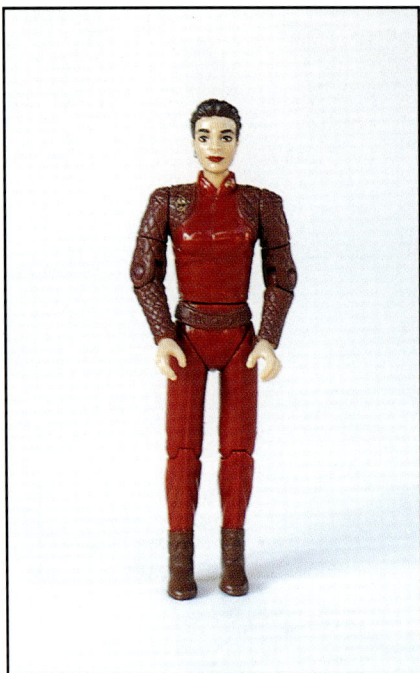

Dr. Julian Bashir
Stock No. 6208
Medical kit
Medical tricorder
PADD
DNA scanner
Type II phaser
Starfleet base
Value: $25.00

Commander Gul Dukat
Stock No. 6207
Cardassian pistol
Cardassian rifle
Cardassian field control unit
Cardassian PADD
Cardassian base
Value: $15.00

Morn
Stock No. 6210
Laser pistol
Pyramid dice
Gold press latinum bars
Exotic beverage glass
Morn base
Value: $15.00

Assort. No. 6070 *The Next Generation* 1994

This series was a continuation of assortment number 6070; but, instead of trading cards some of these figures came with a space cap (pog).

Lt. Cmdr. Data as a Romulan as seen in the episodes *Unification parts I and II*
Stock No. 6031
Romulan rifle
Klingon monitor
Type II phaser
Romulan PADD
Romulan base
Value: $10.00

Lt. Commander LaForge as a Tarchannen III Alien as seen in the episode *Identity Crisis.*
Stock No. 6033
Searchlight
Field kit
UV light source module
Medical monitor kit
Federation base
Value: $10.00

Captain Picard as a Romulan as seen in the episodes *Unification parts I and II.*
Stock No. 6032
Romulan bowl
Romulan disguise kit
Romulan phaser
Romulan PADD
Romulan base
Value: $10.00

Commander Riker as a Malcorian as seen in the episode *First Contact.*
Stock No. 6034
Malcorian medical scanner
Malcorian syringe
Type II phaser
Malcorian monitor
Federation base
Value: $10.00

Lt. Cmdr. Deanna Troi in 6th Season Uniform (green)
Stock No. 6035
Starfleet monitor
Portable computer gear
PADD
Tricorder
Starfleet base
Value: $15.00

Hugh Borg
Stock No. 6037
Mechanical telescoping arm
Power regulator
Scanner device
Borg base
Value: $20.00

Lt. Worf in Starfleet Rescue Outfit as seen in the episode *Birthright I and II.*
Stock No. 6036
Backpack
Klingon spear and ring
Explosive charge
Homing device
Klingon base
Value: $15.00

Dr. Noonian Soong
Stock No. 6038
Human motion simulacrum
Sub-processor
Surgical tool
Crystalline test tubes
Starfleet base
Value: $10.00

Q in Judges Robes
Stock No. 6042
Ceremonial Gavel
Lion Statue
Scroll
Scepter
Q base
Value: $20.00

Lieutenant Barclay
Stock No. 6045
Engineering tool
Anti-gravity pallet
Fencing foil
Cryo canister
Starfleet base
Value: $10.00

Ensign Ro Laren
Stock No. 6044
Tricorder
Type II phaser
Duffel bag
Starfleet monitor
Starfleet base
Value: $25.00

Esoqq member of the Chalnoth race
Stock No. 6049
Knife
Knife leg sheath
Food ration
Chalnoth communicator
Chalnoth base
Value: $70.00

23

Captain Jean-Luc Picard as Dixon Hill as seen in the episode *The Big Good-Bye*.
Stock No. 6050
Pistol
Rotary telephone
Floor lamp
Starfleet base
Value: $20.00

Captain Picard in Duty Uniform
Stock No. 6942
Type II phaser
Mug
Starfleet monitor
Tricorder with holster
Starfleet base
Value: $15.00

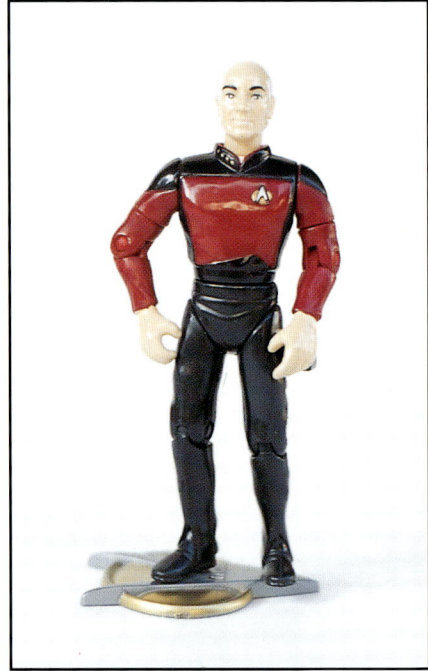

Lt. Commander Data in Dress Uniform
Stock No. 6941
Tricorder
Starfleet monitor
PADD
Plaque of medals
Starfleet base
Value: $15.00

Ensign Wesley Crusher
Stock No. 6943
Engineering scanner
Monitor
PADD
Dilithium crystals
Starfleet base
Value: $15.00

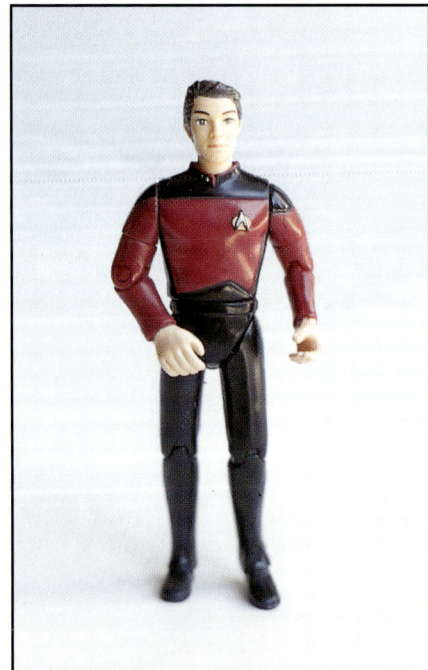

Gowron in Ritual Klingon Attire
Stock No. 6945
Bat'telh
Klingon combat blade
Klingon combat sword
Klingon pain stick
Klingon base
Value: $40.00

Lt. Thomas Riker
Stock No. 6946
Type II Phaser
Portable Computer Gear
Duffel bag
Tricorder with holster
Starfleet base

William Riker's transporter accident other self is a simple repaint of the first series Riker. The tears in the uniform are clearly visible through the paint. Lower numbers of this figure were produced, making it a rather valuable figure. Since it would be very easy to paint a regular Riker, this figure is best kept in its packaging.
Value: $125.00

Assort. No. 6910 *Star Trek Generations* 1994

The *Generations* line actually came out prior to the film. Upon viewing the film, it became apparent Playmates had made a mistake somewhere along the line. The uniforms on the TNG action figures where not in the ones used in the film at all. Also, the scene in which Captain Kirk would have been in a space suit was cut and never seen. The mistake does not increase the value of the figures but it does add to the uniqueness since it is a likeness of something one has never seen in the *Star Trek* universe. With the *Generations* figures, we see the articulation of the figures greatly reduced. The figures do not have knee or elbow joints. This was soon to become a trend with Playmates as more of the *Star Trek* figures would become less articulated.

Admiral James T. Kirk
Stock No. 6911
Classic phaser
Classic communicator
Classic tricorder
Mini movie poster
Generations base
Value: $15.00

Pavel A. Chekov
Stock No. 6916
Classic phaser
Classic communicator
Classic tricorder
Mini movie poster
Generations base
Value: $40.00

Montgomery Scott
Stock No. 6914
Classic phaser
Classic communicator
Classic tricorder
Mini movie poster
Generations base
Value: $40.00

Captain Jean-Luc Picard
Stock No. 6918
Type I phaser
Tricorder
Starfleet monitor
Family album
Mini movie poster
Generations base
Value: $15.00

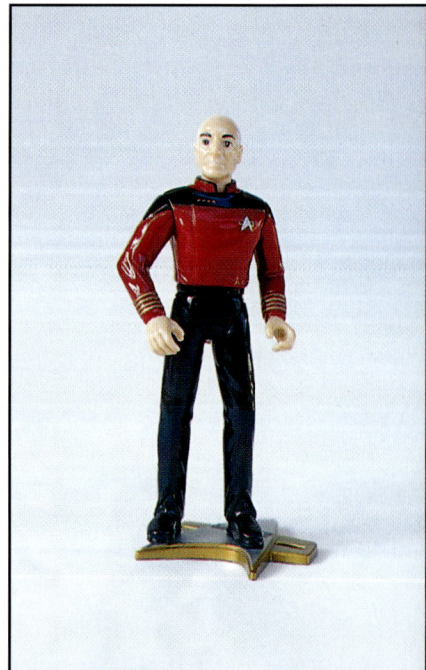

Lieutenant Commander William Riker
Stock No. 6919
Type II phaser
Isolinear chips
Starfleet scanner
Field science kit
Mini movie poster
Generations base
Value: $10.00

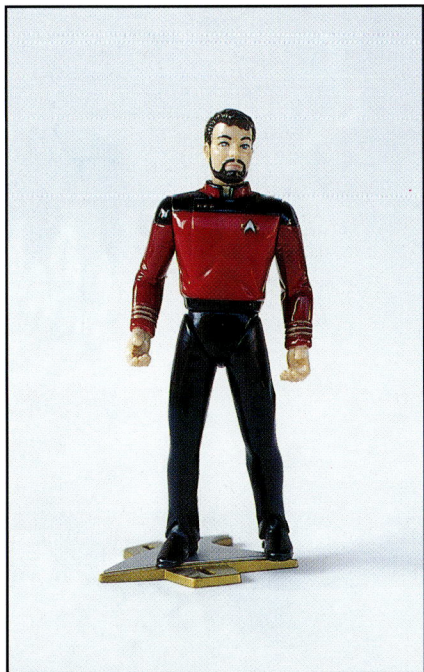

Lieutenant Commander Data
Stock No. 6921
Type II phaser
Tricorder
Starfleet monitor
Isolinear chips
Mini movie poster
Generations base
Value: $10.00

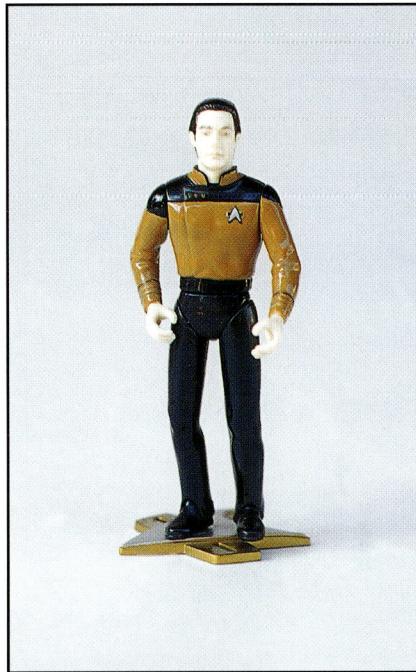

Commander Deanna Troi
Stock No. 6920
Portable computer
Tricorder
Starfleet monitor
PADD
Mini movie poster
Generations base
Value: $12.00

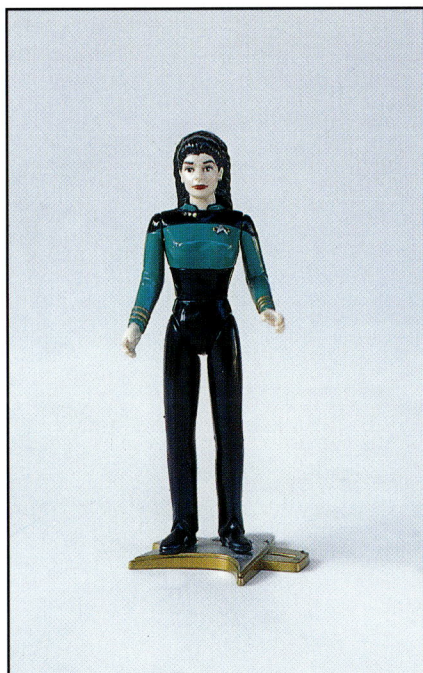

Lieutenant Commander Worf
Stock No. 6922
Type II phaser
UV light source
Tricorder
Phaser rifle
Mini movie poster
Generations base
Value: $10.00

Lieutenant Commander LaForge
Stock No. 6923
Engineering tools
Engineering monitor
Multi-range light source
Isolinear chips
Mini movie poster
Generations base
Value: $10.00

Dr. Soran
Stock No. 6925
Pocket watch
Klingon disruptor
PADD
Multi-range light source
Mini movie poster
Generations base
Value: $15.00

Dr. Beverly Crusher
Stock No. 6924
Medical Tricorder
Type II Phaser
Medical Monitor
Mini movie poster
Generations base
Value: $15.00

Guinan
Stock No. 6927
Tray
Glasses
Starfleet monitor
Mini movie poster
Generations base
Value: $15.00

B'Etor
Stock No. 6928
Klingon ceremonial war club
Klingon disruptor
Klingon knife
Klingon combat sword
Mini movie poster
Generations base
Value: $15.00

Lursa
Stock No. 6929
Ceremonial Klingon sword
Klingon disruptor
Ceremonial Bat'tehl
Isolinear chip
Mini movie poster
Generations base
Value: $15.00

Admiral Kirk in Spacesuit
Stock No. 6930
Champagne Bottle
Engineering tools
Light
Space helmet
Mini movie poster
Generations base
Value: $20.00

Lt. Commander Worf in 19th Century Outfit (also referred to as pirate Worf)
Stock No. 6931
Secret scroll
Swashbuckler's pike
Hand shackle
Pirate sword
Mini movie poster
Generations base
Value: $15.00

Lieutenant Commander LaForge in Movie Uniform

Stock No. 6960
Engineering tools
Monitor
Multi-range light
    source
Isolinear chips
Starfleet Base
Skybox card
Value: $10.00

Lieutenant Commander Data in movie uniform as seen in the film *Generations*

Stock No. 6962
Type II phaser
Tricorder
Monitor
Isolinear chips
Starfleet base
Skybox card
Value: $10.00

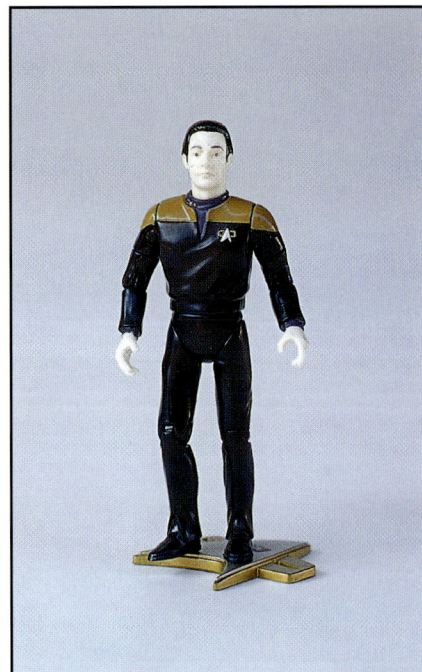

Dr. Beverly Crusher in Starfleet Duty Uniform

Stock No. 6961
Medical tricorder
Medical kit
Type II phaser
Starfleet container
Starfleet base
Skybox card

There are three different combinations of the Starfleet base and the artwork on the package. The basic TNG oval communicator base in the package with the *Generations* base pictured on the back of the package, the same packaging with the *Generations* base inside the package, and the TNG communicator base in the package with the TNG communicator base pictured on the back.
Value: $15.00

Lieutenant Natasha Yar

Stock No. 6965
Type II phaser
Tricorder
PADD
Starfleet issue flashlight
Starfleet base
Skybox card
Value: $12.00

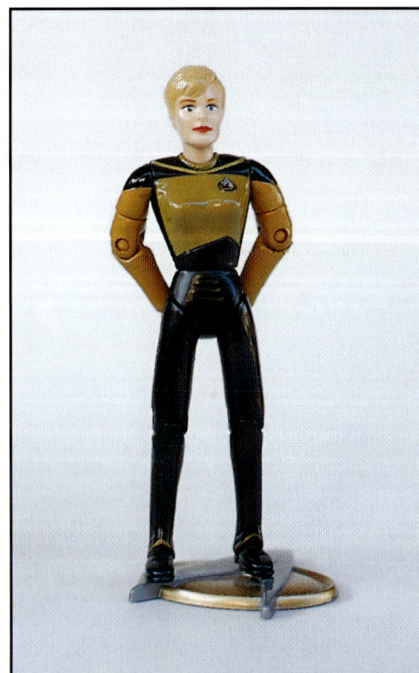

Lwaxana Troi
Stock No. 6967
Wine glass
Crystal gong with mallet
Intergalactic suitcase
Talking gift box
Federation Base
Skybox card
The Canadian version
was released with a
pog instead of the
trading card.
*Value: $10.00; Cana-
dian release w/pog:
$200.00*

The Nausicaan as seen in the episode *Tapestry*
Stock No. 6969
Nausicaan Knife
Telescoping dom-jot cue
Alien bottle
Alien bug
Nausicaan base
Skybox card
Value: $20.00

**Ambassador Sarek Vulcan Ambassador to the United
      Federation of Planets**
Stock No. 6968
Vulcan gong with hammer
Vulcan harp
Vulcan book
IDIC medallion
Vulcan base
Skybox card
The Canadian version was released with a pog instead of
      the trading card.
Value: $10.00; Canadian release w/pog: $200.00

Retired Jean-Luc Picard as seen in the episode *All
      Good Things*
Stock No. 6974
Gardening tools
Scanner
Metal carry case
Skybox card
Starfleet base
    All the figures from the episode *All Good Things* came
with a future communicator base similar to the commu-
nicator pin that was featured in that episode, except the
Picard figure. This figure came with the TNG oval com-
municator base.
Value: $15.00

Lt. Commander Data in 1940s Attire
Stock No. 6979
Holodeck Series
Typewriter
Champagne bottle
Cocktail glass
Skybox card
Starfleet base
Value: $15.00

Ensign Ro Laren
Stock No. 6981
Tricorder
Type II phaser
Duffel bag
Starfleet monitor
Starfleet base
    This is the same figure as 6044 but it is in different packaging and comes with a trading card instead of the pog.
Value: $20.00

Dr. Noonian Soong
Stock No. 6982
Human motion simulacrum
Sub-processor
Surgical tool
Crystalline test tubes
Starfleet base
    This is the same figure as 6038 but it is in different packaging and comes with a trading card instead of the pog.
Value: $10.00

Lt. Worf in Ritual Klingon Attire with metallic armor
Stock No. 6985
Supernova Series
Klingon disruptor
Spiked war club
Pain stick
Skybox card
Klingon base
    The packaging was marked incorrectly for this series. Instead of Supernova Series, it is marked as the Holodeck Series.
Value: $15.00

Captain Jean-Luc Picard as Locutus with metallic armor
Stock No. 6986
Supernova Series
Two electrical enhancement hoses
Two cybernetic Borg hands
Borg base
    The packaging was marked incorrectly for this series. Instead of Supernova Series, it is marked as the Holodeck Series.
Value: $20.00

Assort. No. 6230 *Star Trek DS9* 1995

Each figure in this series came with a space cap (pog).

Commander Benjamin Sisko in dress uniform
Stock No. 6220
DS9 monitor
3D chess set
Starfleet carrying case
Starfleet Base
Value: $15.00

Jake Sisko
Stock No. 6235
Book bag
Baseball mitt
Jum jum stick
DS9 monitor
Base
Value: $20.00

Vedek Bareil
Stock No. 6236
Orb case
Candleholder
Snake in ceremonial encasement
Base
Value: $25.00

Chief Miles O'Brien in Starfleet dress uniform
Stock No. 6226
Cello with bow
Type I phaser
Starfleet carrying case
Pattern enhancer
Base
Value: $10.00

Tosk
Stock No. 6237
Rifle
Collar and leash
Mug
Wormhole action base
Value: $15.00

Lieutenant Jadzia Dax in Duty Uniform
Stock No. 6242
Tricorder
Trill
Field hypospray
Bio sample collector
Portable computer
Base
Value: $15.00

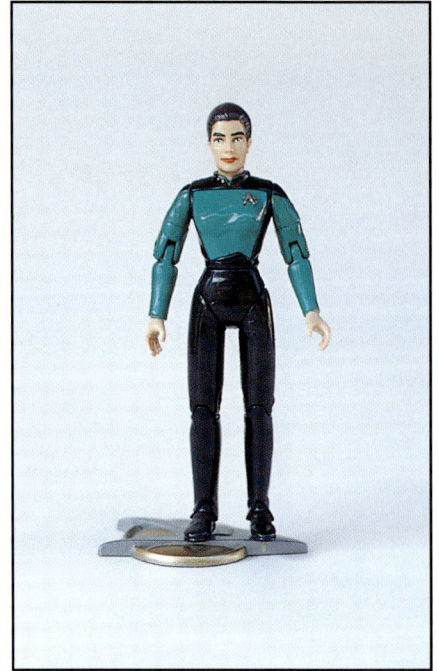

Rom with Nog mini action figure
Stock No. 6241
Lock pick
Magnesite drops
Ferengi base
Value: $20.00

Dr. Julian Bashir in Duty Uniform
Stock No. 6243
Medical kit
Medical tricorder
PADD
DNA scanner
Base
Value: $15.00

Chief Miles O'Brien in Starfleet Duty Uniform
Stock No. 6244
Type II phaser
Engineering kit
Laser drill
Portable fire extinguisher
Base
Value: $10.00

Lt. Thomas Riker in DS9 Uniform
Stock No. 6245
Type II phaser
Tricorder
Scanner
Ds9 monitor
Base
Value: $15.00

Captain Jean-Luc Picard in DS9 Uniform
Stock No. 6245
Type II phaser
Tricorder
Directional UV light source
Field kit
Base
Value: $10.00

Q in DS9 Uniform
Stock No. 6247
Orb case
Type II phaser
PADD
DS9 monitor
Base
Value: $15.00

Assort. No. 6450 Classic *Star Trek* Movie Figures 1995

Each of the five crew members from the *Enterprise* come with a section of the V'GER spacecraft. Once put together, you have a completed V'GER (NASA's Voyager space probe) from TMP.

Admiral James T. Kirk as seen in ST:TMP
Stock No. 6451
Type II phaser
Wrist communicator
PADD
Skybox card
Base
A section of the
 V'GER spacecraft
Value: $10.00

Dr. McCoy
Stock No. 6453 as seen in ST:TMP
Medical tricorder
Medical kit
Neurological scanner
Skybox card
Base
A section of the V'GER spacecraft
Value: $10.00

Commander Spock as seen in ST:TMP
Stock No. 6452
Tricorder
Engineering Tool
Vulcan Kolinahr Necklace
Base
A section of the
 V'GER spacecraft
This figure is the only
 one that did not
 come with a
 trading card.
Valuc: $10.00

Lt. Sulu as seen in ST:TMP
Stock No. 6454
Starfleet phaser
Starfleet wrist
 communicator
Tricorder
Skybox card
Base
A section of the
 V'GER spacecraft
Value: $10.00

Lt. Uhura as seen in ST:TMP
Stock No. 6455
Tricorder
Starfleet wrist communicator
PADD
Skybox card
Base
A section of the V'GER spacecraft
Value: $10.00

Martia as seen in ST:VI *The Undiscovered Country*
Stock No. 6457
Laser Drill
Flare
Drilling mask
Leg irons
Skybox card
Base
Value: $15.00

Khan as seen in ST:II *The Wrath of Khan*
Stock No. 6456
Starfleet phaser
Bowl of Ceti eels
Genesis torpedo
Genesis control box
Skybox card
Base
Value: $10.00

General Chang as seen in ST:VI *The Undiscovered Country*
Stock No. 6458
Klingon communicator
Klingon disruptor
Klingon staff
Glass of Romulan ale
Skybox card
Base
Value: $10.00

Commander Kruge as seen in ST:III *The Search for Spock*

Stock No. 6459
Klingon Communicator
Klingon Tricorder
Klingon Disruptor
Klingon Knife
Skybox card
Base
Value: $10.00

Lt. Saavik as seen in ST:II *Wrath of Khan*

Stock No. 6460
Tricorder
Starfleet phaser
Communicator
Duffel bag
Skybox card
Base
Value: $10.00

Asst. # 6480 Series 1 *Star Trek Voyager* 1995

The Voyager series one figures all came with a Skybox Collector's card of the character from the show.

Captain Kathryn Janeway
Stock No. 6481
Type II phaser
Tricorder
PADD
Desktop monitor
Base
Value: $25.00

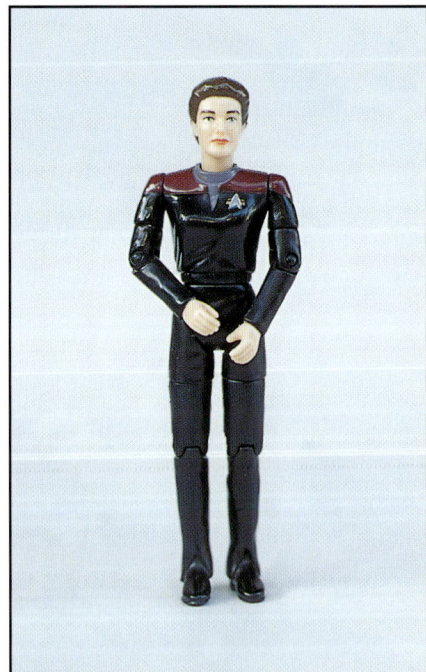

Commander Chakotay
Stock No. 6482
Type II B phaser
Sims beacon
Medicine bundle
Base
Packaging states it comes with a tricorder as well, but it
    does not actually come with one.
Value: $10.00

Lieutenant Tom Paris
Stock No. 6483
Phaser
PADD
Away team gear
Compression phaser rifle
Base
Value: $10.00

Ensign Harry Kim
Stock No. 6484
Tricorder
Field kit
Anti-polaric armband
Polaric generator
Base
　　Early card printings incorrectly printed the descrip-
tion of the tricorder below the picture of the phaser. This
was later corrected.
Value: $10.00

Lieutenant B'Elanna Torres
Stock No. 6485
Phaser
Engineering case
Test cylinder
Trajector device
Base
Value: $20.00

The Doctor
Stock No. 6486
Hypospray
PADD
Desktop monitor
Medical tool
Base
Value: $15.00

Kes the Ocampa
Stock No. 6488
Medical tricorder
PADD
Biological scanner
Desktop monitor
Base
Value: $20.00

Lieutenant Tuvok
Stock No. 6487
Phaser
Tricorder
Sims beacon
Compression phaser rifle
Base
Value: $10.00

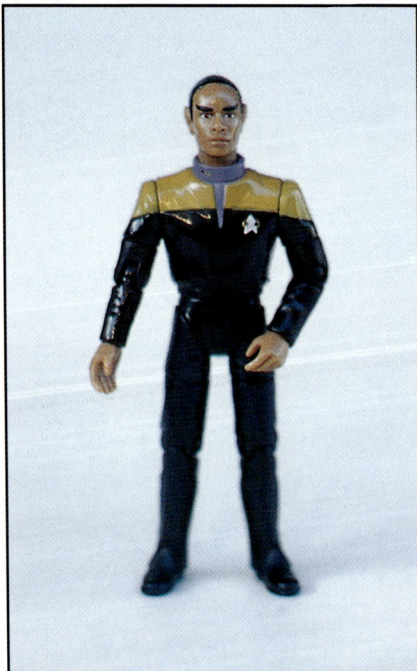

Neelix the Talaxian
Stock No. 6489
Tricorder
Talaxian phaser
Sims beacon
Cooking pan
Base
Value: $15.00

Assort. No. 6430 *Star Trek* all series 1995

For the first time, in this assortment Playmates combined more than one series into an assortment. In this assortment, one will find figures from TOS, TNG, DS9 and Voyager. Also, some of these came with cards, some with pogs, and some without either.

Dr. Katherine Pulaski
Stock No. 6428
Medical scanner
Starfleet monitor
Medical tricorder
Medical case
Base
Value: $15.00

Captain Picard as Galen as seen in the episode *The Gambit*
Stock No. 6432
Stone of Gol
Alien desktop science monitor
Hand disruptor
Alien PADD
Base
Value: $10.00

Vash
Stock No. 6429
Duffel bag
Statue
Dagger
Crystal egg with protective encasement
Federation base
Value: $15.00

Geordi LaForge retired Starfleet officer and journalist as seen in the episode *All Good Things*
Stock No. 6433
Cup of tea
Handheld recorder
Book
Starfleet monitor
Future communicator base
Value: $15.00

Sheriff Worf as seen in the episode *A Fist Full of Datas* with Alexander in western attire mini action figure
Stock No. 6434
Holodeck Series
Two six shooters
Shot glass
Value: $15.00

Dr. Beverly Crusher in 1940s Attire as seen in the episode *The Big Good-Bye*
Stock No. 6435
Holodeck Series
Pistol
Handbag
Parasol
Compact
Base (this figure mistakenly came with a Voyager communicator base)
Value: $15.00

The Traveler
Stock No. 6436
Engineering monitor
Engineering stool
Federation base
Value: $10.00

Governor Worf of H'Atoria as seen in the episode *All Good Things*
Stock No. 6437
Bat'telh
D'k Tahg Knife
Klingon Disruptor
Klingon Monitor
Future communicator base
Value: $10.00

Counselor Deanna Troi as Durango as seen in the episode *A Fist Full of Datas*
Stock No. 6438
Holodeck Series
Sure shot rifle
Six shooter
Ring of jail keys
Showdown time clock
Base
Value: $15.00

The Hunter of Tosk
Stock No. 6439
Rifle
Scanner
Helmet
Wormhole base
Value: $20.00

Lieutenant Jadzia Dax as seen in the episode *Blood Oath*
Stock No. 6440
Bat'telh
D'k Tahg knife
Cup of Bak'Dule
Starfleet duffel bag
Klingon base
Value: $15.00

Borg with spring firing cybernetic arm
Stock No. 6441
Interstellar Action Series
Three Borg entity hoses
Laser scanner
Borg Base
Value: $20.00

Jem 'Hadar
Stock No. 16032
Jem 'Hadar handgun
Jem 'Hadar Rifle
Jem 'Hadar Knife
Wormhole base
Value: $10.00

Lt. Commander Worf in DS9 Uniform
Stock No. 16033
Type II phaser
Klingon battle blade
D'K Tahg
Starfleet duffel bag
Base
Value: $10.00

Admiral William T. Riker as seen in the episode *All Good Things*
Stock No. 16034
Type I phaser
PADD
Desktop monitor
Tricorder
Future communicator base
Value: $10.00

Elim Garak
Stock No. 16035
Tailor's tape measure
Obsidian Order isolinear rods
Cardassian phaser
Cardassian PADD
Cardassian base
Value: $10.00

Mr. Spock as seen in the episode *The Cage*
Stock No. 16038
Hand laser
Communicator
Landing party case
Desktop monitor
Star Trek base
Value: $10.00

Vina as Orion Animal Woman as seen in the episode *The Cage*
Stock No. 16040
Torch
Fountain
Star Trek base
Value: $22.00

The Talosian Keeper as seen in the episode *The Cage*
Stock No. 16039
Nourishment vial
Talosian viewscreen
Gas sprayer
Star Trek base
Value: $15.00

Lt. Natash Yar as seen in the episode *Yesterday's Enterprise*
Stock No. 16043
Isolinear optical chips
Type II phaser
Tricorder
Enterprise-C phaser
base
The YE Yar figure was limited to 3000.
Value: $225.00

Lt. (JG) Reginald Barclay as seen in the *Voyager* **episode** *Projections*
Stock No. 16044
Type II-B phaser
Medical tricorder
Desktop monitor
PADD
This figure was a Limited Edition of 3,000.
Value: $150.00

Assort. No. 16000 Starfleet Academy 1996

Each figure came with a mini-Omnipedia™ Starfleet Academy Files CD-Rom.

Cadet Jean-Luc Picard in standard issue flight training suit
Stock No. 16001
Phaser
Subspace beacon
PADD
Protective flight vest
Eye visor
Starfleet academy base
Value: $10.00

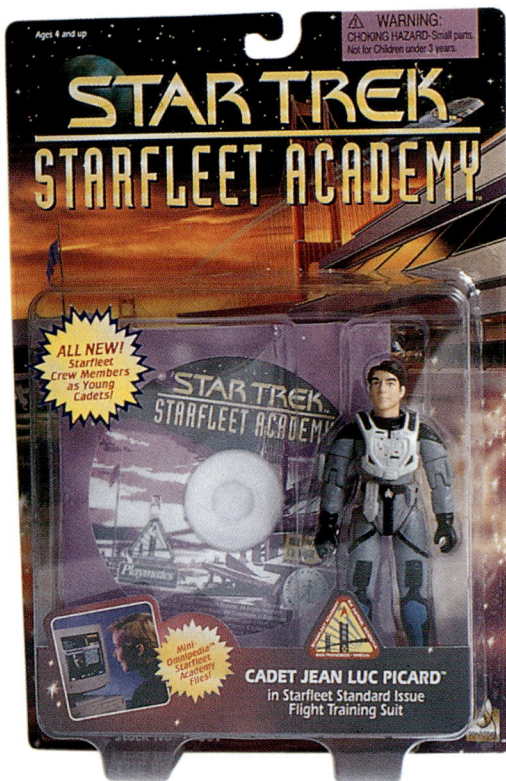

View of packaging with CD ROM and figure.

Cadet Jean-Luc Picard

Cadet William Riker in Geo-Hazard suit
Stock No. 16002
UV light source
Eye visor
Survival pack
Temperature regulator
Starfleet academy base
Value: $10.00

Cadet Geordi LaForge in radiation protection repair suit
Stock No. 16004
Isolinear chips
Carrying case
Chest protector
Diagnostic tool
Starfleet academy base
Value: $10.00

Cadet Worf in night reconnaissance suit
Stock No. 16005
Phaser
Survival knife
Tricorder
Chest protector
Searchlight
Starfleet academy base
Value: $10.00

1996 Series 2 Star Trek Voyager Asst. # 6480

Seska
Stock No. 16460
Type II phaser
Tricorder
Engineering tools
Trajector device
Maquis base
Value: $10.00

Lieutenant Carey
Stock No. 16461
Type II phaser
PADD
Test cylinder
Engineering diagnostic
Base
Value: $10.00

The Kazon
Stock No. 16462
Kazon Rifle
Kazon Canteen
Kazon Hand Gun
Kazon base
Value: $10.00

Torres as a Klingon from the episode *Faces*
Stock No. 16465
Vidiian bioscanner/phaser
Bat'leth
D'k tahg
Klingon ceremonial sword
Klingon base
Value: $10.00

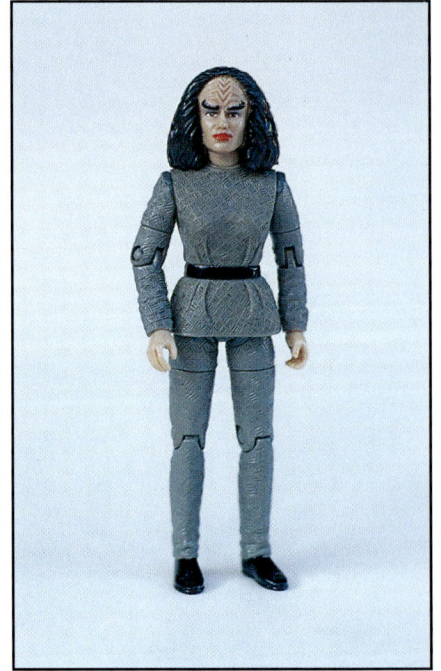

The Vidiian victim of *the Phage*
Stock No. 16463
Vidiian bioscanner/phaser
Medical tricorder
Hypospray
Medical tool
Vidiian base
Value: $10.00

Chakotay as Maquis
Stock No. 16466
Type II phaser
Tricorder
Medical bundle (black birds wing, stone from a river and akoonah)
Maquis base
Value: $8.00

Assort. No. 6430 *Star Trek* all series 1997

Captain Kurn as seen in the *DS9* **episode** *Sons of Mogh*
Stock No. 16020
D'k Tahg knife
Klingon disruptor
Mevak dagger
Adanji
Klingon base
Value: $10.00

Seska as Cardassian as seen in the *Voyager* **episode** *Maneuvers*
Stock No. 16022
Transporter module
DNA tissue sampler
Kazon interrogation device
Kazon communicator
Cardassian base
Value: $8.00

Captain Sisko (bald w/beard)
Stock No. 16021
Type II phaser
Phaser rifle
Interphasic compensator
Desktop computer
Base
Value: $8.00

Tom Paris Mutated as seen in the *Voyager* **episode** *Threshold*
Stock No. 16023
Three mutant offspring
Type II phaser
Base
Value: $8.00

Gorn as seen in the Classic episode *Arena*
Stock No. 16041
Primitive cannon
Diamond projectiles
Stone pike
Metron recorder / translator
Value: $15.00

The Mugato as seen in the Classic episode *A Private Little War*
Stock No. 16042
Flintlock
Mako root
Hill people's drum
Type II phaser
Value: $15.00

Beverly Crusher as seen in the movie *Star Trek: Generations*
Stock No. 16047
Medical tool
Hypospray
Medical kit
Starfleet thermos bottle
Base
This figure was limited to a production run of 10,000.
Value: $35.00

Captain Kirk in Environmental Suit
Stock No. 16048
Classic tricorder
Classic phaser
Desktop monitor
Tri-Ox compound
Base
Value: $10.00

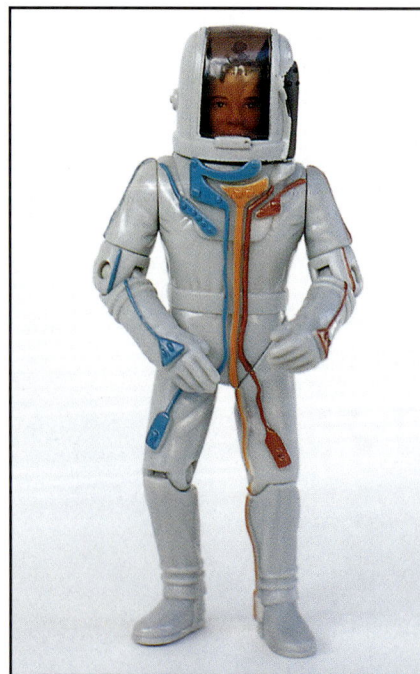

Professor Data as seen in the episode *All Good Things*
Stock No. 16152
Tea cup
Tea kettle
Tray
Vase
Future communicator base
Value: $10.00

Harry Mudd as seen in the episode *Mudd's Women"*
and "I, Mudd
Stock No. 16154
Goblet
Lithium crystals
Venus drug
Communicator
Base
Value: $12.00

Dr. McCoy in Dress Uniform as seen in the episode
Journey to Babel
Stock No. 16155
Tricorder
Hypospray
Communicator
Anabolic protoplaster
Base
This figure was limited to an edition of 10,000.
Value: $35.00

Assort. No. 65100 Warp Factor Series 1 *DS9* 1997

This is the first of the Warp Factor Series. This series of figures either came with or without fuzzy tribbles in the package with the figure. The fuzzy tribbles were actually only small pompoms. Each figure also came with a *Triple Tribbles* game piece. Figures with the fuzzy tribbles are valued slightly higher than those without.

Chief Miles O'Brien as seen in the episode *Trials and Tribble-ations*
Stock No. 65106
Engineering tool
Two tribbles
Classic tricorder
Classic communicator
Base
This figure had a limited release of only 10,000.
Value: $50.00

Lt. Commander Jadzia Dax as seen in the episode *Trials and Tribble-ations*
Stock No. 65108
Medical equipment
Two tribbles
Electronic clipboard
Classic tricorder
Base
Value: $12.00

Captain Benjamin Sisko as seen in the episode *Trials and Tribble-ations*
Stock No. 65107
Orb of time
Two tribbles
Electronic clipboard
Classic communicator
Base
Value: $8.00

Constable Odo as seen in the episode *Trials and Tribble-ations*
Stock No. 65109
Orb of time
Two tribbles
Bomb scanner
Classic tricorder
Base
Value: $8.00

Dr. Julian Bashir as seen in the episode *Trials and Tribble-ations*
Stock No. 65110
Hypospray
Two tribbles
Classic tricorder
Classic communicator
Base
Value: $8.00

Captain Koloth as seen in the episode *Trials and Tribble-ations*
Stock No. 65110
Three tribbles
Klingon disruptor pistol
D'k tahg
Klingon Base
Value: $10.00

Assort. No. 65100 Warp Factor Series 2 *All Star Trek* 1997

Sisko as Klingon as seen in the episode *Apocalypse Rising*
Stock No. 65101
Klingon bloodwine cup
Polaron emitter
Klingon Bat'leth
Klingon disruptor pistol
Klingon base
Value: $8.00

Ilia Probe
Stock No. 65102
Comes with all five pieces when assembled forms a complete V'Ger.
    Base
Value: $10.00

Leeta the Dabo Girl
Stock No. 65103
Dabo wheel
Two bars of latinum
Bajoran base
Value: $15.00

Swarm Alien
Stock No. 65104
Two Swarm rifles
Swarm base
Value: $10.00

Captain Beverly Crusher Picard as seen in the episode
    All Good Things
Stock No. 65112
Bonsai tree
Optical medical tool
Hypospray
PADD
Future communicator
Value: $10.00

Assort. No. 65100 Warp Factor Series 3 *All Star Trek* 1997

Spock as seen in the episode *Mirror Mirror*
Stock No. 65105
Desktop computer
Agonizer
Mirror universe phaser
Knife
Base
Value: $8.00

Cadet Deanna Troi
Stock No. 65115
Data recorder
Sample collector
Backpack
Starfleet phaser
Starfleet Academy base
Value: $8.00

Edith Keeler as seen in *City on the Edge of Forever*
Stock No. 65114
Coffee pot
Hand bag
Typewriter
Coffee mug
Star Trek Base
Value: $7.00

Cadet Data
Stock No. 65116
Scanner
Starfleet phaser
Bio sensor
Sample collector
Starfleet Academy base
Value: $8.00

Cadet Beverly Howard Crusher
Stock No. 65117
Bio sensor
Sample analyzer
Medical tool belt
Radiation mask
Starfleet Academy base
Value: $8.00

Assort. No. 65140 Warp Factor Series 4 *All Star Trek* 1998

Andorian as seen in the episode *Whom Gods Destroy*
Stock No. 65120
Ultrasound Neutralizer
Andorian Scrape
Star Trek base
Value: $10.00

Keiko O'Brien
Stock No. 65121
Desktop monitor
Starfleet thermal bottle
Type II phaser
Base
Value: $10.00

Trelane
Stock No. 65122
Mirror machine
Sword
Pistol
Star Trek base
Value: $8.00

Intendant Kira
Stock No. 65124
Bajoran pistol
Bajoran rifle
Desktop monitor
Bajoran base
Value: $50.00

Kang as seen in episode *Blood Oath*
Stock No. 65123
Klingon Bat'leth
Klingon disruptor
Mevax dagger
Klingon base
Value: $10.00

James Kirk as seen in the episode *The City on the Edge of Forever*

Stock No. 65128
Phaser
Mug
Coffee pot
Base
Value: $10.00

Mr. Spock as seen in the episode *The City on the Edge of Forever*

Stock No. 65129
Cup for coffee
Primitive computer
Vacuum tubes
Value: $10.00

Borg Queen as seen in the movie *Star Trek: First Contact*

Stock No. 65130
Mechanical arm
Power regulator
Scanner
Borg base
The Queen's body separates.
Value: $15.00

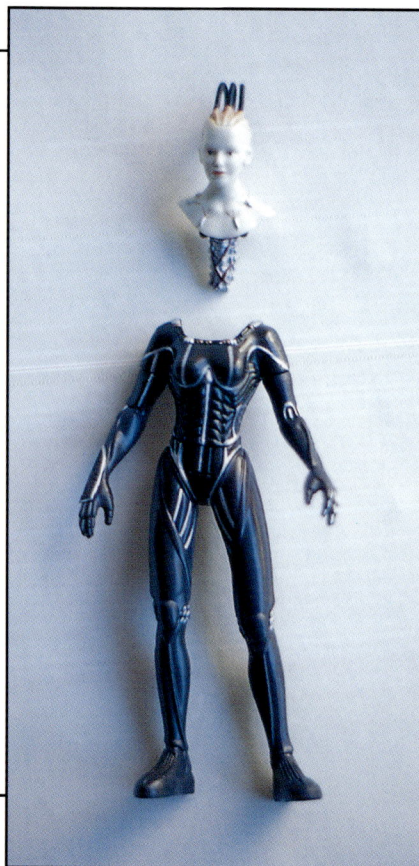

The Queen Borg separated.

Borg Seven of Nine as seen in *Star Trek: Voyager* episode *The Gift*
Stock No. 65131
Scaner
Power regulator
Borg alcove
Borg base
Value: $15.00

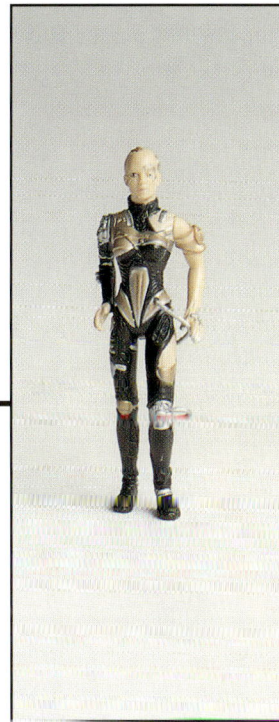

Assort. No. 65400 Transporter Series I *The Original Series* 1998

Each of the Transporter Series figures comes with a TOS electronic light and sound base. With just a push of a button one can hear the transporter sound and the base lights up. Each figure is semi transparent with glitter throughout to give it that *beaming* effect.

Front of the Transporter Series packaging.

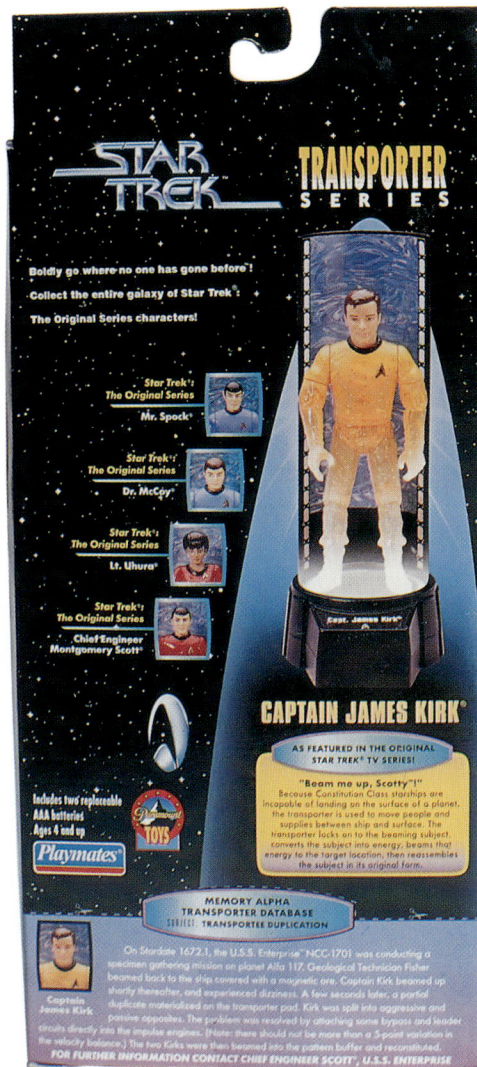

Back of the packaging.

Captain James T. Kirk
Stock No. 65401
Value: $12.00

Transporting Kirk

Dr. McCoy
Stock No. 65403
Value: $12.00

Transporting McCoy

Mr. Spock
Stock No. 65402
Value: $12.00

Transporting Spock

Lt. Uhura
Stock No. 65404
Value: $12.00

Transporting Uhura

Lt. Scott
Stock No. 65404
Value: $12.00

Transporting Scotty

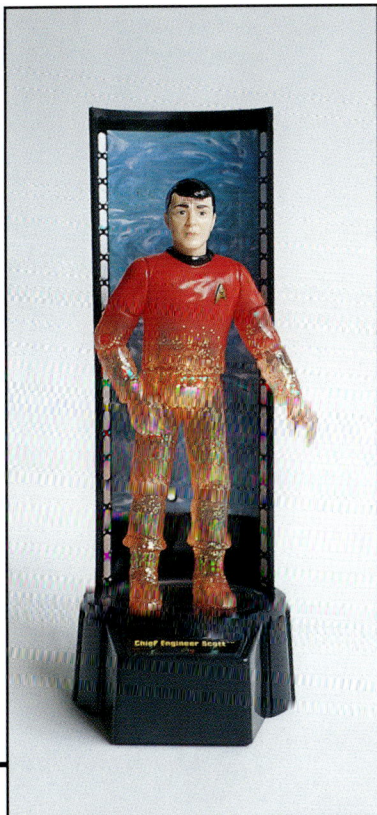

Captain Jean-Luc Picard
Stock No. 65422
Value: $12.00

Transporting Picard

Assort. No. 65400 Transporter Series *The Next Generation* 1998

Each of the Transporter Series figures comes with a TNG electronic light and sound base. With just a push of a button one can hear the transporter sound and the base lights up. Each figure is semi-transparent with glitter throughout to give it that *beaming* effect.

Lt. Commander Data
Stock No. 65421
Value: $12.00

Transporting Data

Lt. Worf
Stock No. 65423
Value: $12.00

Transporting Worf

Commander William T. Riker
Stock No. 65432
Value: $12.00

Lt. Commander Geordi LaForge
Stock No. 65433
Value: $12.00

Transporting Riker

Transporting LaForge

Exclusives and Special Figures

JC Penney's Exclusive

Lt. Commander Data in red uniform as seen in the episode *Redemption*

Stock No. 6947
Portable tractor beam
Tricorder with holster
Starfleet science kit
Hand laser

This figure was sold exclusively through the JC Penney's 1993 catalog along with three other figures. The other three figures were Picard in duty uniform, Wesley Crusher and Deanna Troi. Data in his red uniform was never seen in the episode *Redemption*.
Value: $195.00

Spencer's Gifts Exclusives

Assort. No. 6430 Convention Exclusives from Spencer's 1996

These two figures were originally only available at the *One Weekend On Earth* Convention in Huntsville, Alabama. After the convention they were also briefly available from Spencer's through mail order. Each figure was limited to a production run of 10,000 pieces.

Lt. Commander Montgomery Scott as seen in the pilot episode *Where No Man Has Gone Before*

Stock No.16045   Classic phaser
Classic tricorder   Engineering base
Classic communicator   *Value: $30.00*

Photo courtesy of Jon (Bart of Borg) Huss.

Lt. Hikaru Sulu as seen in the pilot episode *Where No Man Has Gone Before*
Stock No. 16046
Classic tricorder
Classic communicator
Classic phaser
Science Base
Value: $30.00

Assort. No. 65267 Spencer's Exclusives 1997

With a limited release of only 10,000 of each figure. Spenser's first offered these figures as a mail order only item. However, they soon became available in the stores instead of through the mail.

Lt. Commander Jadzia Dax
Stock No. 65268
Type II phaser
Risaen perfume
Zhian' tara pitcher
Zhian' tara candle
Base
Value: $12.00

Security Officer Neelix
Stock No. 65269
PADD
Type II phaser
SIMS beacon
Cooking pan
Value: $12.00

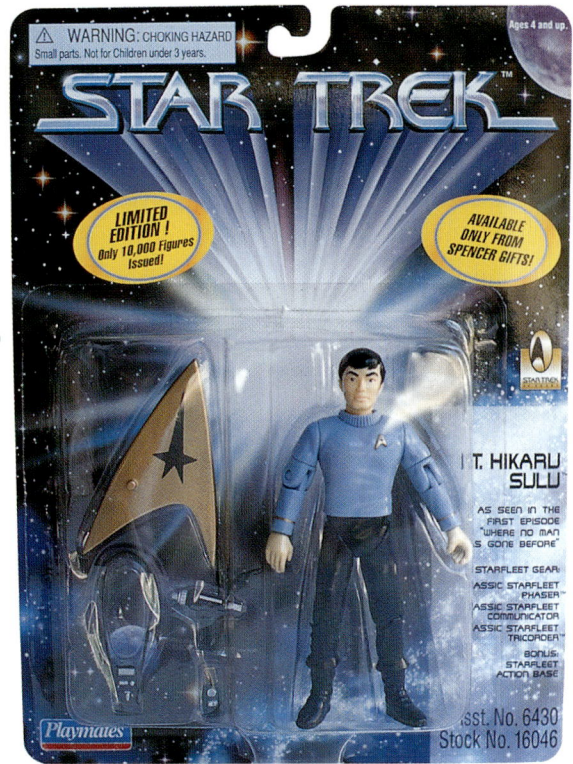

Mail-away Sisko

This figure was an exclusive mail-away offer from Playmates Interactive in 1995. Available only with the purchase of the *Deep Space Nine: Crossroads of Time* game for either Super Nintendo or Sega Genesis. There were only 4000 of these figures produced. Sisko did not come with any accessories or a base. Value: $80.00

Paramount Pictures Exclusives

Worf Return To Grace Collection
Stock No. 16145

Lt. Cmdr. Worf came packaged with the Worf Return to Grace Video Collection in 1997. There were no accessories with the figure. Playmates made 40,000 of these figures for this video collection.
Value: $60.00

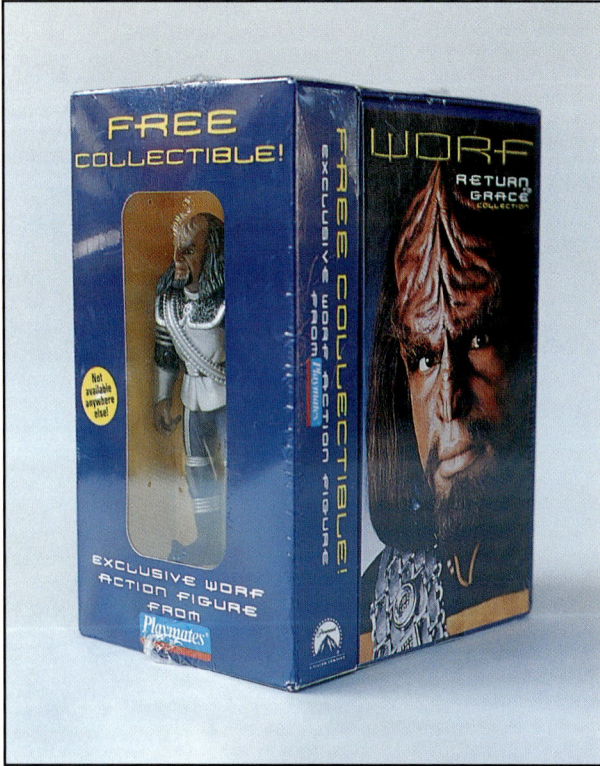

Viacom Exclusives

Trifold Borg
Two cybernetic arms
Borg hoses
Borg base

This figure was never publicly available, but was given out as a Viacom promotional piece. Most likely to possible licensees as the packaging lists the names and addresses of U.S. and international contacts. The trifold borg has a copyright date of 1996, coinciding with the theatric release of *Star Trek: First Contact*.
Value: $600.00

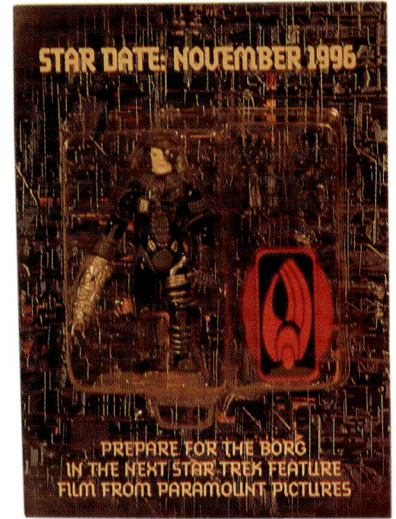

Trifold Borg from the private collection of Dean Andrade. *Photo taken by Dean Andrade.*

Target Exclusives

Assort. No. 65230 Transporter Series *The Original Series* 1998

There were only 10,000 of each of these figures produced. As with the other Transporter Series figures, each figure comes with an electronic base with lights and sounds. Other than the base, there were no other accessories for these figures.

Ensign Pavel Chekov
Stock No. 65231
Value: $18.00

Lt. Hikaru Sulu
Stock No. 65232
Value: $18.00

Yeoman Janice Rand
Stock No. 65442
Value: $18.00

Assort. No. 65440 Transporter Series *The Original Series* 1999

As with the other Transporter Series figures, each figure comes with an electronic base with lights and sounds. Other than the base, there were no other accessories for these figures. These two figures are part of Target's Starfleet Command Series with instructions on how to enter the sweepstakes.

Nurse Christine Chapel
Stock No. 65441
Value: $18.00

Assort. No. 65800 *ST:TNG* 1999

There were only 10,000 of each of these figures produced.

Captain Jean-Luc Picard in movie uniform as seen in the ST:TNG films
Stock No. 65801
Phaser rifle
Tricorder
Borg scanner
Type II phaser
Base
Value: $12.00

Lt. Commander Worf in movie uniform as seen in the ST:TNG films
Stock No. 65802
Bat'leth
Type II phaser
D'K Tahg knife
Tricorder
Base
Value: $12.00

Assort. No. 65620 Star Trek Starfleet Command Series Only Available at Target 1999

There were only 10,000 of each of these figures produced.

Seven of Nine in silver outfit from *Voyager*
Stock No. 65803
Phaser rifle
Scanner
Desktop monitor
Base
Value: $15.00

Data in movie uniform as seen in the ST:TNG films
Stock No. 65804
Tricorder
Type II phaser
Phaser rifle
Engineering case
Base
Value: $12.00

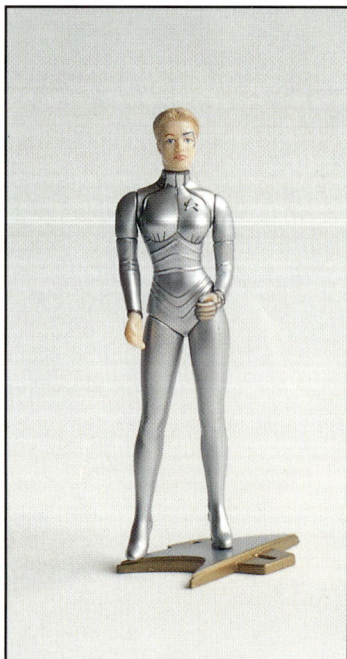

Toyfare Magazine Exclusives

Toyfare and Wizard magazines offered exclusive figures for sale through their magazines. The figures are the same except for the packaging and the fact that Gareb Shamus, the publisher, also signed the Wizard figures.

Tapestry II Picard in science officer uniform as seen in the episode *Tapestry*.
Stock No. 65276
The figure came in a plain white box with the Toyfare and Wizard logos on it. It did not come with any accessories other than a phaser.
Value: $20.00

Translucent Geordi LaForge as a Tarchannen III alien as seen in the episode *Identity Crisis*.

Stock No. 65277

This figure also came in a basic white box with the Toyfare and Wizard logos on it. Accessories for this figure are a UV light source and a Federation base.

Value: $20.00

Transporting Tasha Yar comes with a base and a phaser.

Stock No. 65279

This figure is partially transparent like the other transporter figures but does not come with an electronic base.

Value: $18.00

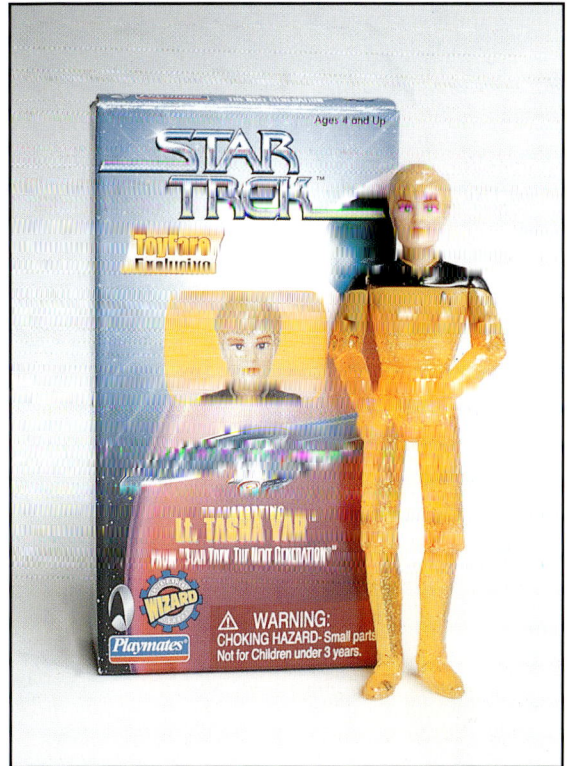

Mr. Spock in environmental suit as seen in the episode *The Tholian Web*.

Stock No. 65278

We see a packaging change with this figure. Mr. Spock comes with a tricorder and base.

Value: $20.00

Captain James T. Kirk as a gangster as seen in the episode *A Piece of the Action* comes with a base and communicator.
Value: $15.00

Toyfare exclusive Kirk in packaging.

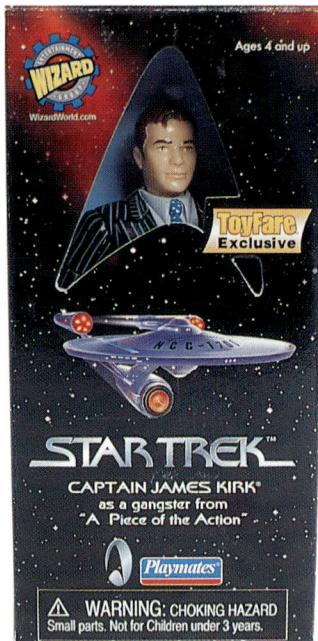

Gangster Kirk from Toyfare.

New Force Comics Exclusive

Kathryn Janeway as seen in the *Voyager* episode *Flashback*
Stock No. 65226
Flashback Janeway was limited to only 10,000 pieces.
Value: $12.00

Star Trek Fan Club Exclusive

Captain Mackenzie Calhoun
Stock No. 65221
Sword
Base

This was the fan club's first exclusive figure. Captain Calhoun is the first (and only) *Star Trek* figure created from a never before seen character. The character of Captain Calhoun is not from a television series. He is from the *ST: New Frontier* book series by Pocket Books.
Value: $8.00

4.5 Inch Multi-packs and Boxed Sets

Stock No. 6090 *Classic Star Trek* **Bridge Set 1993**

The crew of the USS Enterprise NCC-1701 are displayed in the box as if they are on the bridge of *The Enterprise*. The *Classic Star Trek* Bridge Set consists of seven figures from the Original Series: Captain James T. Kirk, Mr. Spock, Ensign Pavel Chekov, Lt. Sulu, Lt. Uhura, and Lt. Cmdr. Montgomery Scott. Each figure comes with a communicator, phaser and base.
Value: $50.00

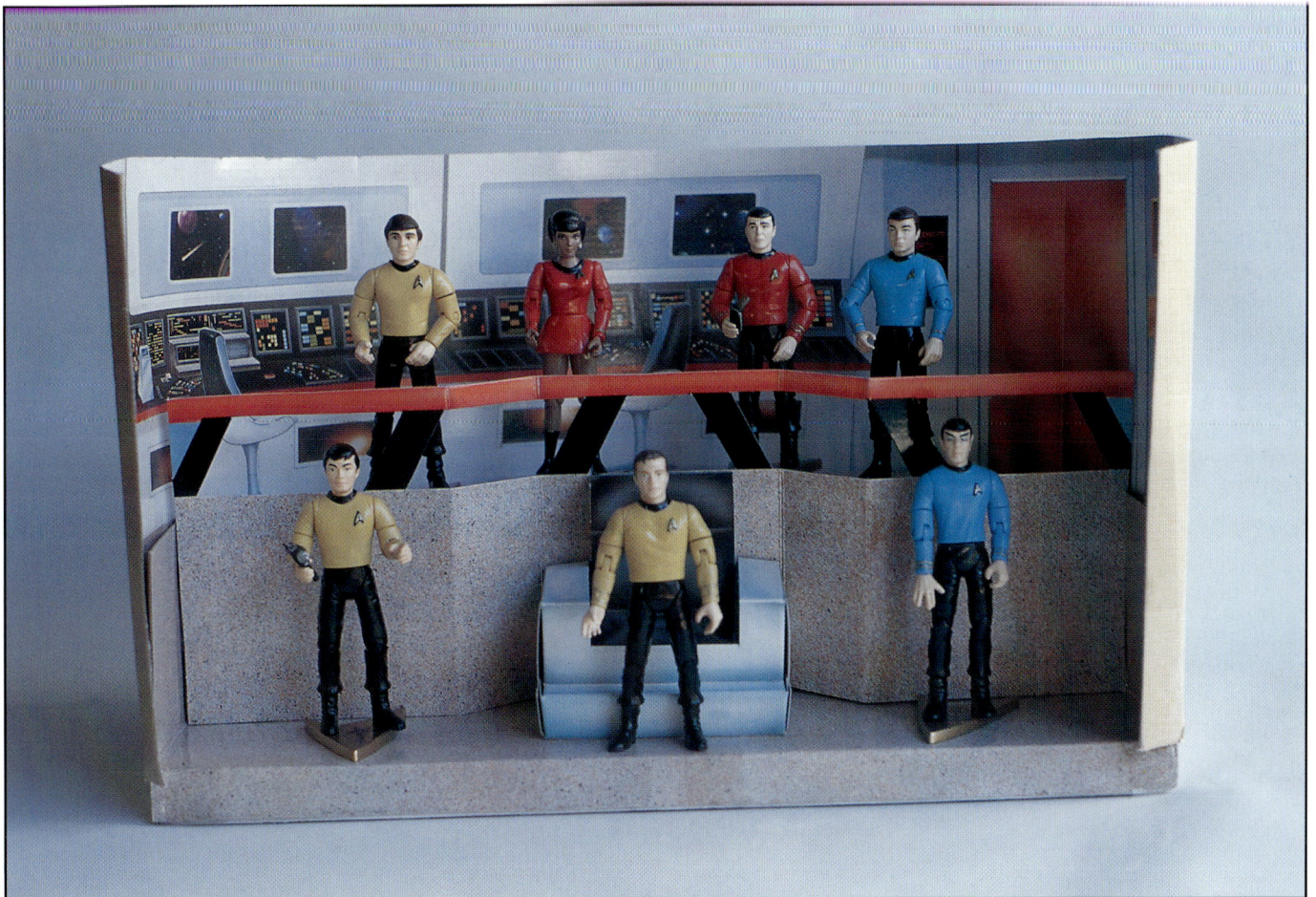

Stock No. 16122 1701 Collector Series 3 Pack 1998

   After Playmates had released these three figures as limited editions, many of the collector's wanted them but could not since only 1701 figures had been produced. This unique three pack had the same three figures as the original individual figures but allowed the general public a chance to get figures previously out of reach.
Value: $25.00

Lt. Natasha Yar as seen in the episode *Yesterdays Enterprise*
Isolinear optical chips
Enterprise C phaser
Type II phaser
Tricorder
Captain Jean-Luc Picard as seen in the episode *Tapestry*
Drinking mugs
Dom-jot stick
Duffel bag
Chess set
Lt. Reginal Barclay as seen in the episode *Projections*
Medical tricorder
Type II phaser
PADD
Desktop monitor

Assort. No. 65180 Twin Packs 1998

Picard as Dixon Hill and Guinan as Gloria as seen in the *TNG* episode *Clues*
Stock No. 65181
Holodeck Series
Comes with a Dixon Hill display environment.
Value: $20.00

Kirk with Balok and Balok's Puppet as seen in the
TOS **episode** *The Corbomite Maneuver*
Stock No. 65182
Alien Series
Comes with an alien display environment.
Value: $20.00

Assort. No. 65190 Twin Packs 1999

Lt. Cmdr. Data, Lt. Worf and Alexander Rozhenko as
seen in the *TNG* **episode** *A Fistful of Datas*
Stock No. 65191
Holodeck Series
Comes with a diorama display environment featuring a
scene from that episode.
Value: $20.00

Ensign Harry Kim and Species 8472 as seen in the *Voy-*
ager **episode** *Scorpion*
Stock No. 65192
Alien Series
Comes with a display environment.
Value: $20.00

4.5 Inch Multi-Pack Exclusives

Toys R Us Exclusives

Stock No. 6190 Starfleet Officers Collectors Set 1994
Three legendary commanders and their first officers were available for the first time. A collector's note on the back of the package reads: "Captain Kirk, Mr. Spock, Captain Picard, and Commander Riker figures are attired in their dress uniforms and available here for the first time." The collectors numbering is on the box and not on each individual figure, just like with the Classic Bridge Set. This set comes with a deluxe action base that holds all six figures. *Value: $20.00*

Captain James T. Kirk in dress uniform and Mr. Spock in dress uniform.
Legendary Captain and first officer of the *USS Enterprise NCC-1701*
 Both figures come with a classic communicator and a classic phaser.
Captain Jean-Luc Picard in dress uniform and Commander William Riker in dress uniform.
Famous Captain and first officer of the *USS Enterprise NCC-1701-D*
 Figures come with tricorder, type I, type II phasers and Starfleet monitor.
Commander Benjamin Sisko and Major Kira Nerys
Leader and first officer of *Deep Space Nine*
 Kira comes with a Bajoran phaser and a Bajoran tricorder while Cmdr. Sisko comes with a phaser rifle and a DS9 monitor.

Starfleet Command Twin Pack 1999

Borg Drone and Captain Jean-Luc Picard as Locutus of Borg as seen in the *TNG* episode *The Best of Both Worlds*
Stock No. 65173
Alien Series
Comes with a display environment from that episode.
Value: $25.00

Captain James Kirk in interphase and Mister Spock as seen in the *TOS* episode *The Tolian Web*
Stock No. 65174
Comes with a display environment from that episode.
Value: $25.00

6 Inch Figures

Asst. # 16100 6" Figures from *Star Trek: First Contact* 1996

Captain Jean-Luc Picard
Stock No. 16101
Starfleet type II phaser
Compression phaser rifle
PADD
Borg scanner
Mini movie poster
Base
Value: $8.00

Commander William T. Riker
Stock No. 16102
Starfleet type II phaser
Compression phaser rifle
Tricorder
Sims Beacon
Mini movie poster
Base
Value: $8.00

Lt. Commander Geordi LaForge
Stock No. 16103
Engineering case
Engineering monitor
Engineering tools
Starfleet type II phaser
Mini movie poster
Base
Value: $8.00

Lt. Commander Data
Stock No. 16104
Starfleet tricorder
Starfleet type II phaser
Laser drill
Test cylinder
Mini movie poster
Base
Value: $8.00

Lt. Commander Worf
Stock No. 16105
Starfleet type II phaser
Compression phaser rifle
D'k Tahg
Desktop monitor
Mini movie poster
Base
Value: $8.00

Commander Deanna Troi
Stock No. 16106
Away team case
Shot glass
PADD
Starfleet type II phaser
Mini movie poster
Base
Value: $8.00

Dr. Beverly Crusher
Stock No. 16107
Medical tricorder
Hypospray
Biological scanner
Medical tool
Mini movie poster
Base
Value: $8.00

The Borg
Stock No. 16108
Borg scanner
Surgical grafting tool
Mini movie poster
Base
Value: $10.00

Zefram Cocrane
Stock No. 16109
Engineering kit
Maintenance tool
Liquid refreshment
Flashlight
Mini movie poster
Base
Value: $8.00

Lily
Stock No. 16110
Starfleet type II phaser
DNA scanner
Searchlight
Biosample collector
Mini movie poster
Base
Value: $8.00

Picard in Starfleet Spacesuit
Stock No. 16115
Starfleet type II phaser
Compression phaser rifle
Helmet
Mini movie poster
Base
Value: $10.00

Assort. No. 16250 Combat Action Series Warp Factor Series 1 *TNG* 1997

Captain Jean-Luc Picard with "real" fencing action
Stock No. 16251
Sword
Phaser rifle with projectile
Type II phaser
Klingon D'K Tahg knife
Base
Value: $10.00

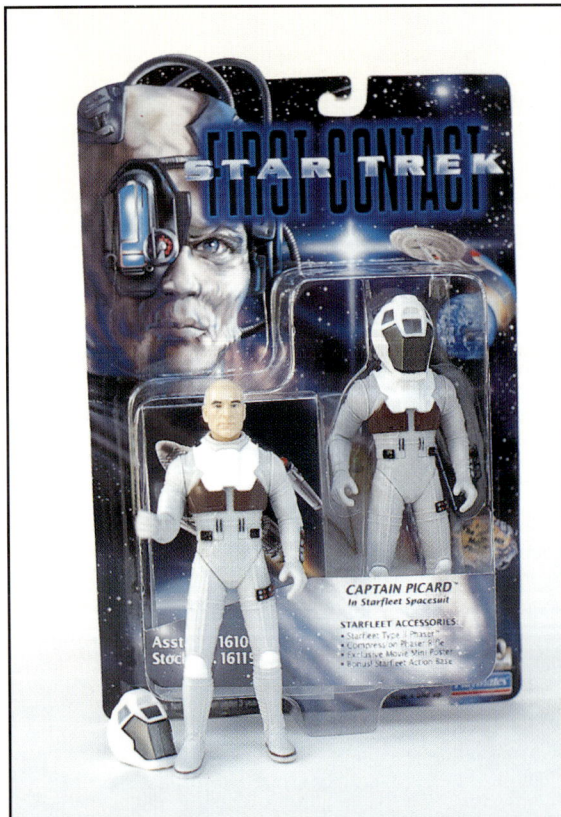

Commander William T. Riker with "real" phaser drawing action
Stock No. 16252
Phaser rifle with
    projectile
Type II phaser
Tricorder
Sims beacon
Base
Value: $10.00

Lt. Commander Worf with "real" Bat'leth slashing action
Stock No. 16253
Klingon Bat'leth
Disruptor
Mek'leth
D'K Tahg knife
Knife
Base
Value: $10.00

Q with "real" fencing action
Stock No. 16255
Sword
Pirates musket
Pike
Pirate's sword
Q base
Value: $10.00

Borg with spring-firing Borg arm
Stock No. 16254
Cybernetic arm projectiles
Surgical tool
Borg scanner
Base
Value: $10.00

Cardassian Soldier
Stock No. 16256
Cardassian tactical station
Cardassian phaser
The tactical station has plastic sides and a printed cardboard front and top.
Value: $8.00

Jem 'Hadar Soldier
Stock No. 16257
Jem 'Hadar engineering console which consists of four plastic columns.
Value: $8.00

Captain Benjamin Sisko
Stock No. 16258
USS Defiant Captain's chair
The chair is made of all plastic with a snap together design.
Value: $8.00

Lt. Commander Jadzia Dax
Stock No. 16260
USS Defiant helm console
Console consists of a plastic top with applied stickers and a folded cardboard base.
Value: $8.00

Chief Miles O'Brien
Stock No. 16266
USS Defiant engineering station
Station consists of a plastic top and a folded cardboard base.
Value: $8.00

7 Inch Figures

Assort. No. 6080 Space Talk Series *TNG* 1995

There are four different figures in this series. Each figures says three different phrases and comes with an adventure booklet.

Captain Jean-Luc Picard
Stock No. 6081
PADD
Type I phaser
"Damage Report"
"Engage"
"Captain's log supplemental"
Value: $10.00

Commander William Riker
Stock No. 6082
Tricorder
Type II phaser
"Energize"
"Shields up"
"Red alert"
Value: $10.00

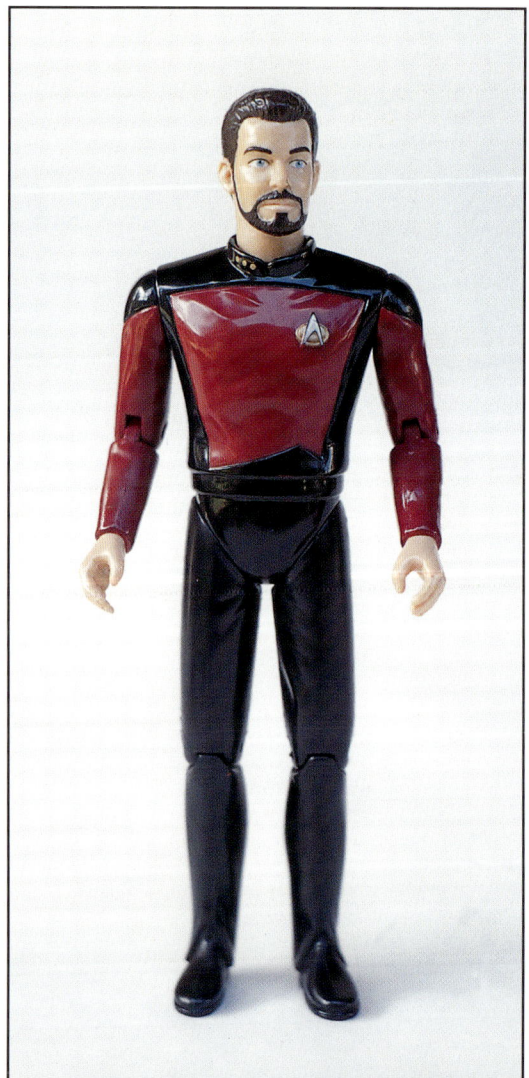

Borg
Stock No. 6085
Borg connector tubes
Borg scanner
"We are the Borg"
"You must comply"
"Freedom is irrelevant"
Value: $20.00

Q
Stock No. 6086
Q continuum scepter
Ceremonial gavel
"Bonjour mon Capitan"
"What a pity"
"Humans"
Value: $20.00

View of the push button activated voice on the Space Talk Series.

Captain James T. Kirk
Stock No. 6142
Type II phaser
Champagne bottle
Multi-range light source
Mini movie poster
Base
Value: $80.00

Lieutenant Commander Geordi LaForge
Stock No. 6144
Accessories.
Engineering Kit
Engineering Tools
Tricorder
Mini movie poster
Base
Value: $30.00

Lieutenant Commander Data
Stock No. 6143
Tricorder
Type II phaser
Ultra violet light source
Mini movie poster
Base
Value: $30.00

Generations LaForge. *Courtesy of Pagoda Comics.*

Assort. No. 6280 Collector Series 1995

This series of figures came with an exclusive space cap (pog) from Skybox.

Borg
Stock No. 6069
Alien Edition
Collective connector tubes
Borg base
Value: $30.00

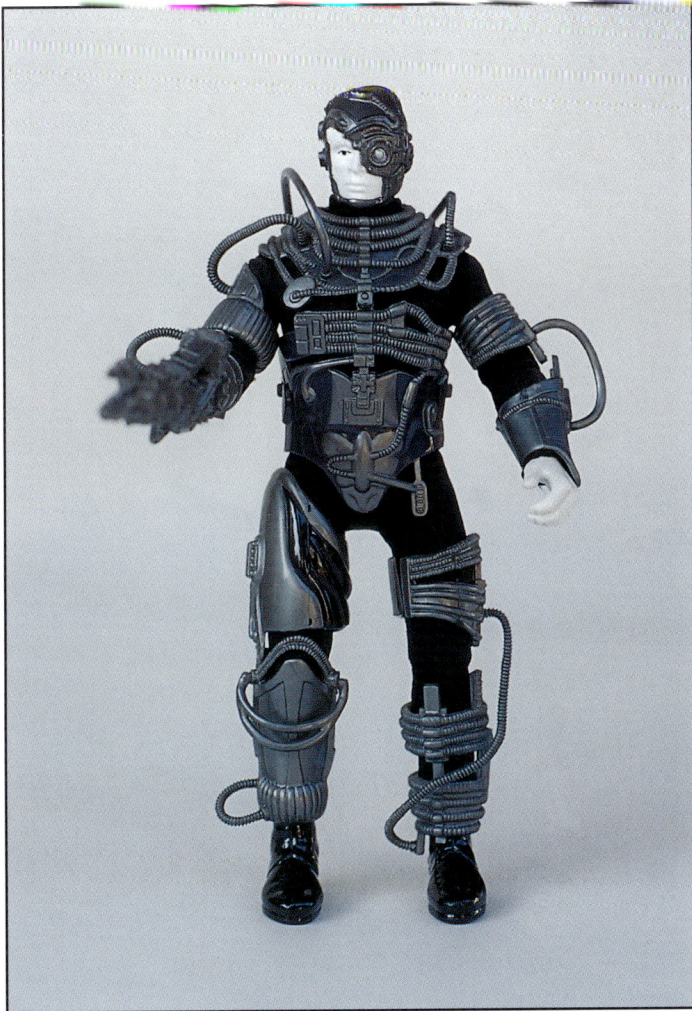

Commander Deanna Troi
Stock No. 6281
Starfleet Edition
PADD
Portable computer gear
Tricorder
Base
Value: $40.00

Dr. Beverly Crusher
Stock No. 6282
Starfleet Edition
Hypospray
Medical tricorder
Medical kit
Base
This figure can be found with or without a plastic band around her head to control her wild hair.
Value: $45.00

Guinan
Stock No. 6283
Federation Edition
Two drinking glasses and tray
Base
Value: $35.00

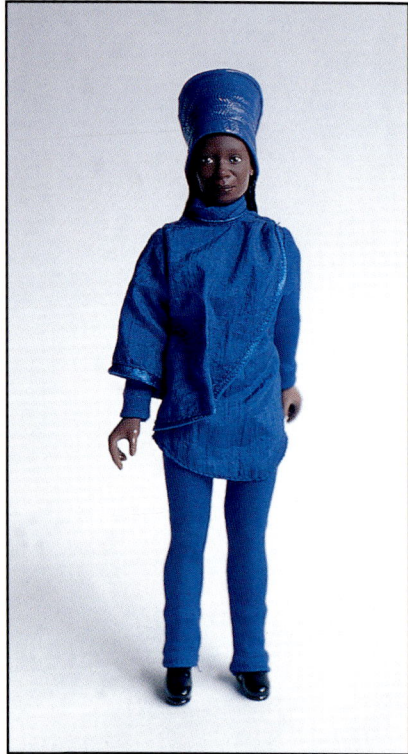

Commander William Riker
Stock No. 6285
Starfleet Edition
Phaser rifle
UV light source
Type II phaser
Base
Value: $25.00

Lieutenant Commander Data
Stock No. 6284
Starfleet Edition
Tricorder
Laser light
Isolinear chips
Base
Value: $25.00

Lieutenant Worf in Ritual Klingon Attire
Stock No. 6286
Alien Edition
Bat'telh
Klingon disruptor
Klingon knife
Klingon base
Value: $40.00

Lieutenant Commander Geordi LaForge
Stock No. 6287
Starfleet Edition
PADD
Tricorder
Multi-range light source
Base
Value: $25.00

Captain James T. Kirk in Dress Uniform
Stock No. 6288
Classic tricorder
Classic communicator
Classic phaser
Starfleet base
Value: $35.00

Photo courtesy of Jon (Bart of Borg) Huss.

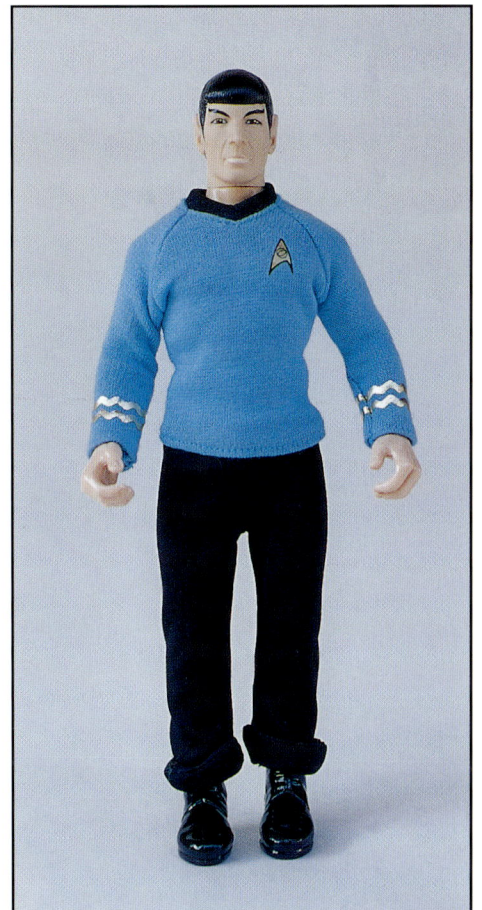

Captain Jean-Luc Picard in Dress Uniform
Stock No. 6289
Type I phaser
Tricorder
PADD
Value: $30.00

Mr. Spock
Stock No. 6291
Federation Edition
Classic tricorder
Classic phaser
Vulcan harp
Base
Value: $40.00

Chief Medical Officer Dr. Leonard McCoy
Stock No. 6292
Federation Edition
Test tubes
Tricorder
Communicator
Base
Value: $30.00

**Assort. No. 6280
Collector Series 1996**

Lt. Cmdr. Montgomery Scott
Stock No. 6293
Federation Edition
Phaser
Multi-range light
   source
Engineering tool
Base
Value: $25.00

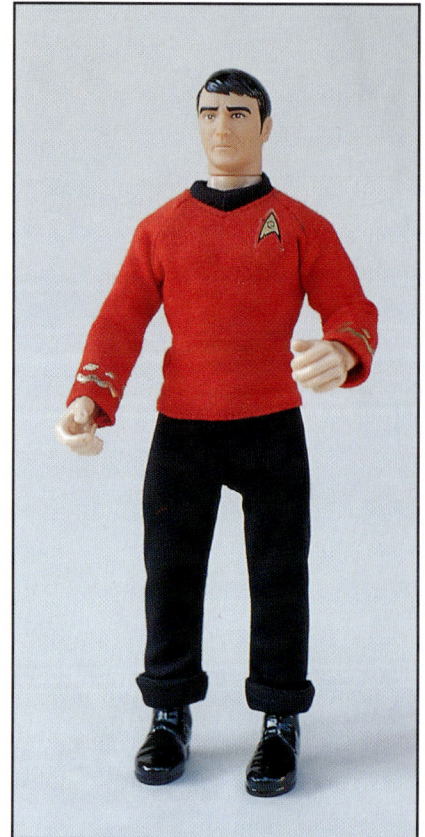

Lt. Uhura
Stock No. 6294
Starfleet Edition
Phaser
Tricorder
Communicator
Base
Value: $40.00

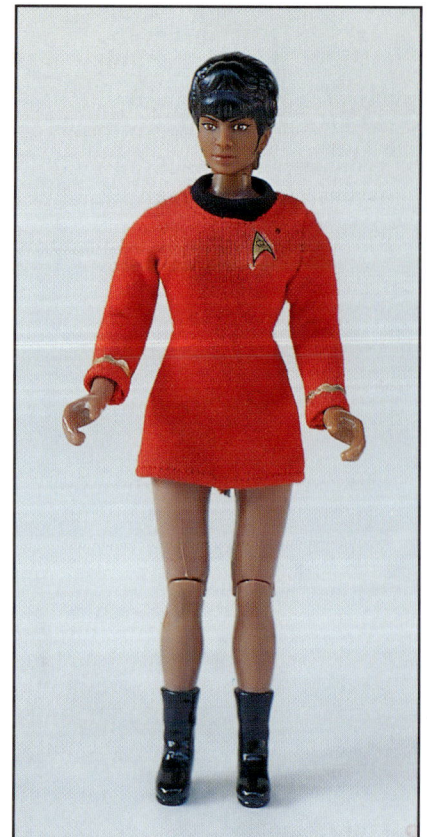

Lt. Cmdr. Worf in DS9 Uniform

Stock No. 6295
Bat'telh
Starfleet phaser rifle
Tricorder
Starfleet base
Value: $25.00

Photo courtesy of Jon (Bart of Borg) Huss.

Chief Engineer Miles O'Brien

Stock No. 16182
Federation Edition
Type II phaser
Multi-range light source
Base
Value: $15.00

Romulan Commander

Stock No. 16181
Alien Edition
Romulan disruptor rifle
Romulan disruptor
Romulan PADD
Romulan base
Value: $25.00

Captain Christopher Pike

Stock No. 16183
Federation Edition
Hand laser (which is actually a phaser)
Communicator
Tricorder
Base
Value: $20.00

Q in Judges Robes
Stock No. 16187
Alien Edition
Staff
Lion head statue
Gavel
Q base

    There are two different variations of this figure. One with an unpainted face and one with a painted face. The painted face has a glossy finish while the unpainted face has a flat matte finish.
Value unpainted: $25.00; Painted: $35

Q with unpainted face.

Q with a glossy painted face.

Captain Benjamin Sisko in Dress Uniform
Stock No. 16188
Federation Edition
Starfleet type II Phaser
Compression Phaser Rifle
Desk Top Monitor
Value: $20.00
Courtesy of Pagoda Comics

Major Kira Nerys
Stock No. 16189
Bajor Edition
Bajoran phaser
Bajoran tricorder
Bajoran PADD
Bajoran base
    There are several different variations of this figure. The ridges on the nose are either painted or unpainted. The belt has three different variations as well; circles cut out of the belt, circles painted on the belt, or slashes painted on the belt.
Value: $30.00

Kira with paint nose ridges and painted circles on her belt.

Kira with unpainted nose ridges and circular holes in her belt.

Assort. No. 65280 Warp Factor Series 1 1997

This series came with the Triple Tribbles Game cards and some of the figures came with large fuzzy tribbles.

Constable Odo
Stock No. 65281
Bajoran tricorder
Bajoran PADD
DS9 computer interface terminal
Bajoran base
Value: $20.00; w/tribbles: $35.00

Commander Chakotay
Stock No. 65286
Type II phaser
Medicine bundle which contains a blackbird's wing, a stone from a river, and an akoonah.
Starfleet base
Value: $25.00

Lt. Tuvok
Stock No. 65283
Sims Beacon
Phaser rifle
Base
Value: $25.00

Assort. No. 65280 Warp Factor Series 2 *Voyager* 1997

Captain Kathryn Janeway
Stock No. 65282
Type II phaser
Tricorder
PADD
Base
Value: $40.00

Lt. Tom Paris
Stock No. 65285
Starfleet away team gear
Phaser rifle
Starfleet base
Value: $15.00

Jem 'Hadar Soldier
Stock No. 65290
Jem 'Hadar rifle
Hand gun
Knife
Wormhole base
Value: $20.00

Gul Dukat
Stock No. 65291
Cardassian pistol
Cardassian field control unit
Cardassian PADD
Cardassian rifle
Cardassian base
Value: $20.00

Dr. Julian Bashir
Stock No. 65286
Tricorder
Medical kit
DNA scanner
Value: $20.00

Captain Kirk in Casual Attire as seen in the episode
Trouble with Tribbles
Stock No. 65292
Phaser
Two tribbles
Communicator
Starfleet base
Value: $20.00

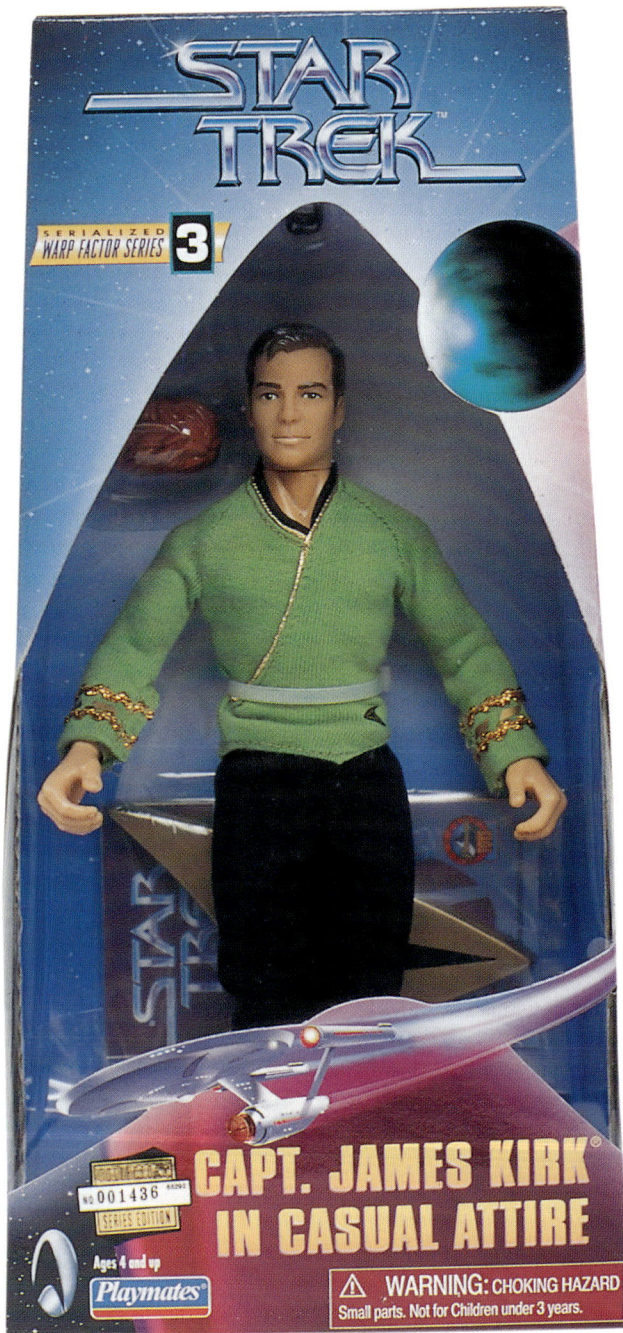

Assort. No. 65280 Warp Factor Series 4 1998

Captain Benjamin Sisko as seen in the episode *Trials and Tribble-ations*
Stock No. 65293
Classic communicator
Two tribbles
Classic phaser
Classic base
Value: $20.00

Lt. Commander Jadzia Dax as seen in the episode *Trials and Tribble-ations*
Stock No. 65294
Classic communicator
Two tribbles
Classic tricorder
Classic base
Value: $40.00

Seven of Nine in silver biosuit
Stock No. 65303
Borg alcove
Borg base
Value: $40.00

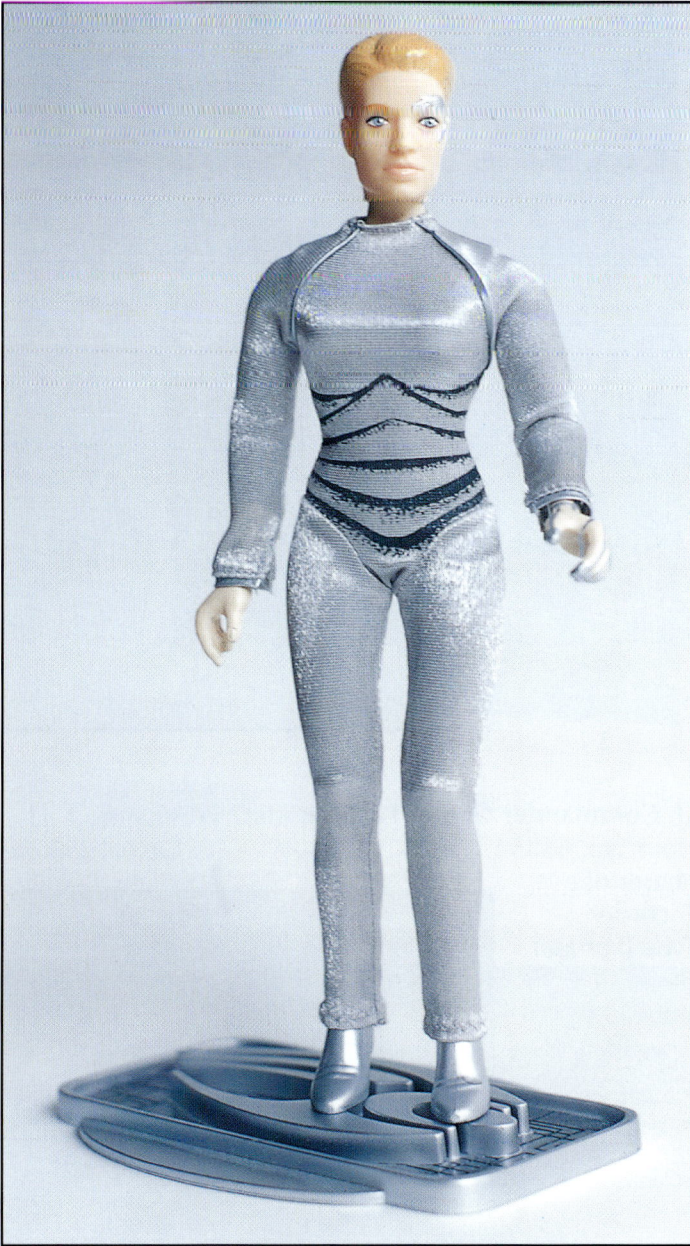

Talosian as seen in the episode *The Cage*
Stock No. 65295
Talosian viewer with image of Christopher Pike on it
Starfleet base
Value: $25.00

Elim Garak
Stock No. 65297
Cardassian PADD
Cardassian phaser
Cardassian field control unit
Cardassian rifle
Cardassian base
Value: $20.00

Anij
Stock No. 65358
Type II phaser
Starfleet rations
Ba'ku base
Value: $20.00

Assort. No. 65390 Alien Combat Series 1999

This series of oversized muscle-bound aliens was sculpted for Playmates by Art Asylum.
There is no special collectors numbering on these figures.

Borg Drone.

Klingon Warrior.

Borg Drone with no accessories
Stock No. 65391
Value: $25.00

Front of the Borg package.

Back of the Borg package.

Klingon Warrior with Bat'leth
Stock No. 65391
Value: $25.00

Back of the Klingon package.

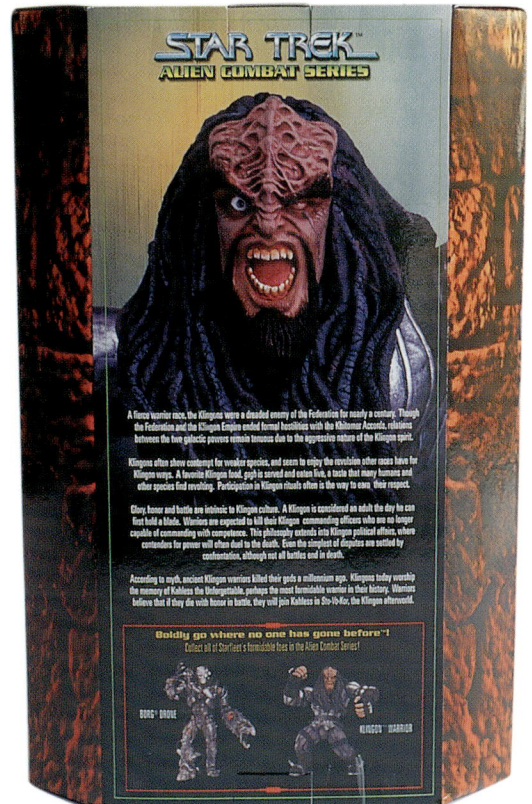

Front of the Klingon package.

Assort. No. 16090 Kaybee Toys Exclusives 1996

The *Piece of the Action* figures were limited to 5000 of each figure.

James T. Kirk as seen in the episode *A Piece of the Action*
Stock No. 16091
Machine gun
Starfleet communicator
Starfleet phaser
Value: $115.00

Mr. Spock as seen in the episode *A Piece of the Action*
Stock No. 16092
Machine gun
Starfleet communicator
Starfleet phaser
Value: $115.00

Courtesy of Pagoda Comics.

Courtesy of Pagoda Comics.

Assort. No. 65259 Kaybee Toys Exclusive 1997

James T. Kirk as seen in the episode *City on the Edge of Forever*
Stock No. 65260
Classic communicator
Classic tricorder
Classic phaser
Starfleet base
Limited to 6500 of each figure.
Value: $70.00

Spock as seen in the episode *City on the Edge of Forever*
Stock No. 65261
Classic communicator
Classic tricorder
Classic phaser
Starfleet base
Value: $70.00

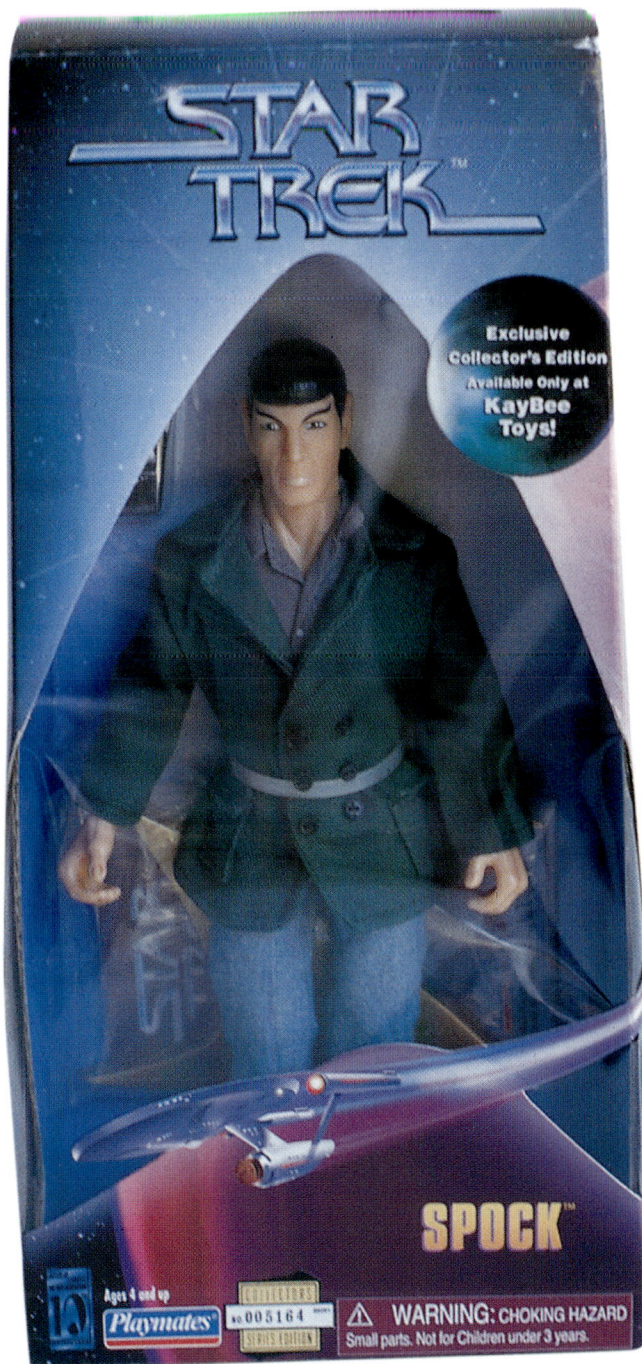

Assort. No. 65210 KB Toys Exclusives 1998

Both the Kirk and Spock figures are limited to 7200 pieces each.

Captain James Kirk as seen in the episode *Mirror Mirror*
Stock No. 65211
Mirror universe agonizer
Mirror universe knife
Starfleet phaser
Mirror universe base
Value: $50.00

Mr. Spock as seen in the episode *Mirror Mirror*
Stock No. 65212
Mirror universe agonizer
Mirror universe knife
Starfleet phaser
Mirror universe base
Value: $50.00

Assort. No. 65200 KB Toys Exclusives 1998

This series of *Mirror Mirror* figures was also limited to only 7200 pieces for each figure.

Dr. McCoy as seen in the episode *Mirror Mirror*
Stock No. 65201
Mirror universe agonizer
Mirror universe knife
Starfleet phaser
Mirror universe base
Value: $45.00

Lieutenant Uhura as seen in the episode *Mirror Mirror*
Stock No. 65202
Mirror universe agonizer
Mirror universe knife
Starfleet phaser
Mirror universe base
Value: $45.00

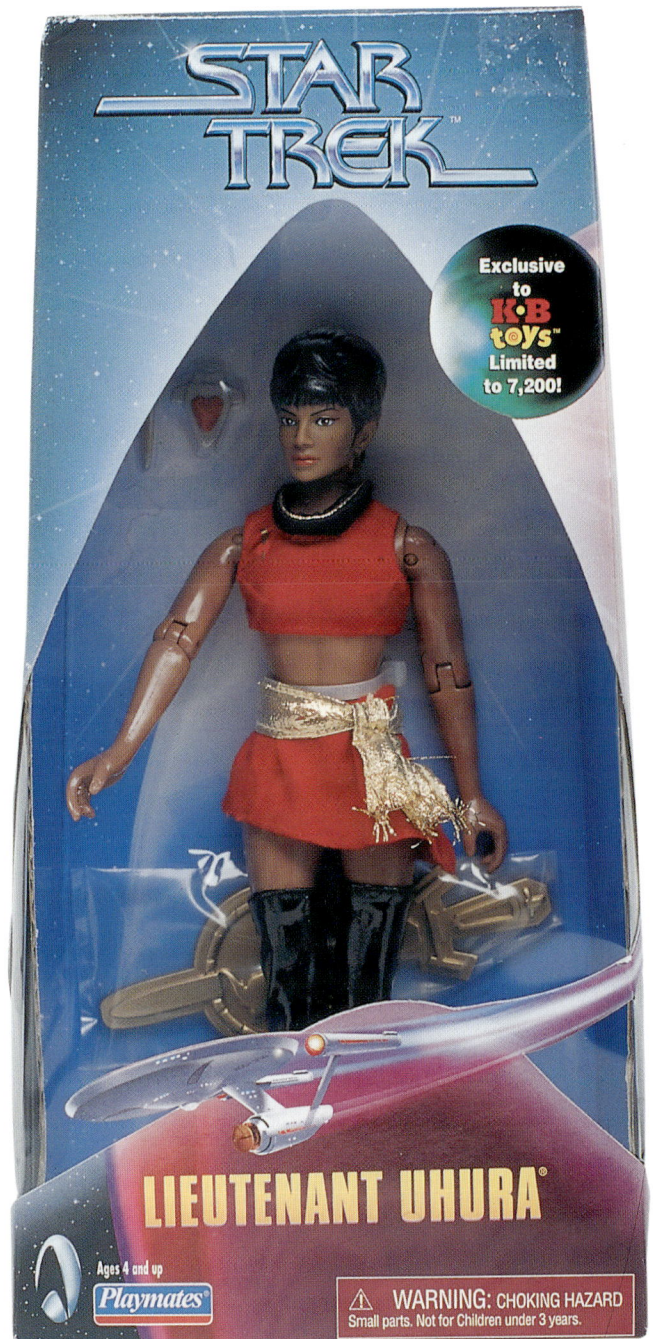

Assort. No 65263 Spencer Gifts Exclusive First Season Uniforms 1997

Figures were limited to a production of only 6000 of each character.

Captain Picard in first season uniform
Stock No. 65264
Desktop monitor
Tricorder
Type II phaser
Base
Value: $35.00

Commander William Riker in first season uniform
Stock No. 65265
Starfleet rifle tricorder
Type II phaser
Value: $35.00

Assort. No. 16095 Target Exclusives 1996

James T. Kirk as seen in the episode *Where No Man Has Gone Before*

Stock No. 16096
Communicator
Tricorder
Phaser
Base
Value: $35.00

Lt. Cmdr. Montgomery Scott as seen in the episode *Where No Man Has Gone Before*

Stock No. 16098
Phaser
Multi-range light source
Engineering diagnostic tool
Base
Value: $35.00

Mr. Spock as seen in the episode *Where No Man Has Gone Before*

Stock No. 16097
Communicator
Phaser
Vulcan harp
Base
Value: $35.00

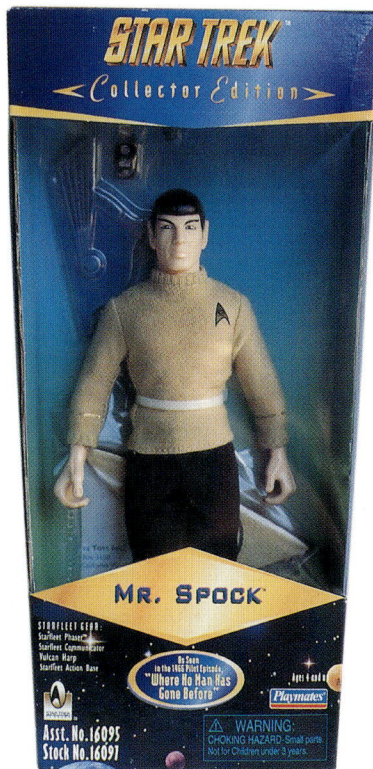

Lieutenant Hikaru Sulu as seen in the episode *Where No Man Has Gone Before*

Stock No. 16099
Phaser
Communicator
Tricorder
Base
Value: $35.00

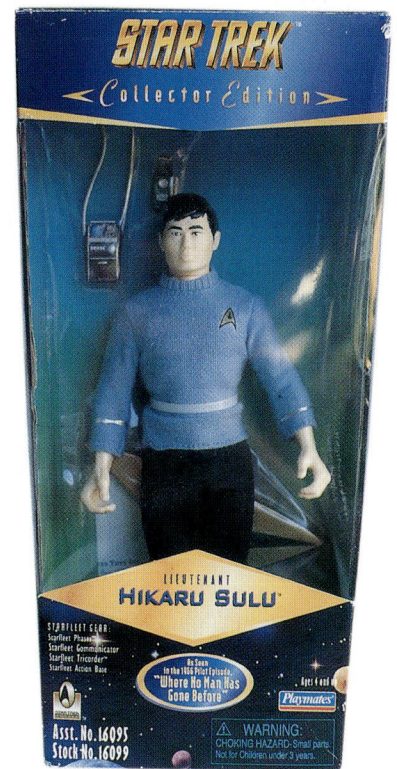

Assort. No. 65255 Target Exclusives 1997

Holographic Doctor the EMH (Emergency Medical Hologram)
Stock No. 65256
Hypospray
Medical tool
Medical tricorder
Starfleet base
Value: $30.00

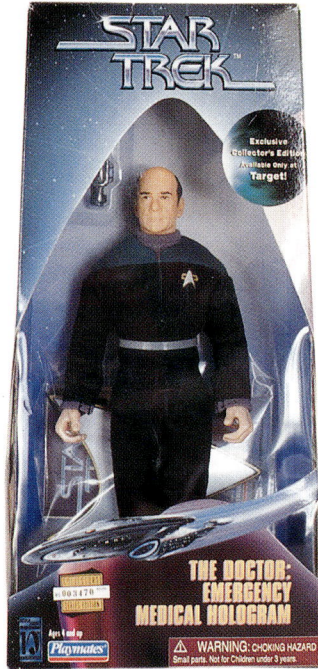

Photo courtesy of Jon (Bart of Borg) Huss.

Ensign Harry Kim
Stock No. 65257
Polaric generator
Anti-polaric armband
Tricorder
Starfleet base
Value: $30.00

Photo courtesy of Jon (Bart of Borg) Huss.

Assort. No. 65250 Target Exclusive from *The Tholian Web* 1998

Mr. Spock in Environmental Suit as seen in the episode *The Tholian Web*
Stock No. 65251
Communicator
Phaser
Base
Value: $30.00

Ensign Chekov in Environmental Suit as seen in the episode *The Tholian Web*
Stock No. 65252
Communicator
Phaser
Base
Value: $30.00

Kirk in Environmental Suit as seen in the episode *The Tholian Web*

Stock No. 65601
Phaser
Communicator
Starfleet base
Value: $30.00

Seven of Nine in brown suit

Stock No. 65602
Borg alcove
Starfleet phaser
Borg base
Value: $40.00

Nurse Christine Chapel
Stock No. 65603
Medical tricorder
Test tubes
Communicator
Base
Value: $30.00

Captain Jean-Luc Picard in Starfleet jacket
Stock No. 65604
Tricorder
Type II phaser
Base
Value: $30.00

Assort. No. 65630 Target Exclusive 1999

Lt. Cmdr. Data as Sherlock Holmes as seen in the episode *Elementary, Dear Data*
Stock No. 65605
Meerschaum pipe
Magnifying glass
Stradivarius violin
Base
Value: $30.00

Lt. Geordi LaForge as Dr. John Watson as seen in the episode *Elementary, Dear Data*
Stock No. 65606
Dairy and ink pen
Base
Value: $30.00

Assort. No. 65070 *Star Trek: Insurrection* 1998

Captain Jean-Luc Picard as seen in the film *Star Trek: Insurrection*
Stock No. 65071
PADD
Disintegrator Bazooka
Value: $30.00

Lt. Commander Worf as seen in the film *Star Trek: Insurrection*
Stock No. 65073
Bat' leth
Phaser
Value: $30.00

Cmdr. William Riker as seen in the film *Star Trek: Insurrection*
Stock No. 65072
Phaser rifle
PADD
Tricorder
Value: $30.00

Lt. Commander Data as seen in the film *Star Trek: Insurrection*
Stock No. 65074
Phaser
Tricorder
S'ona rifle
Value: $30.00

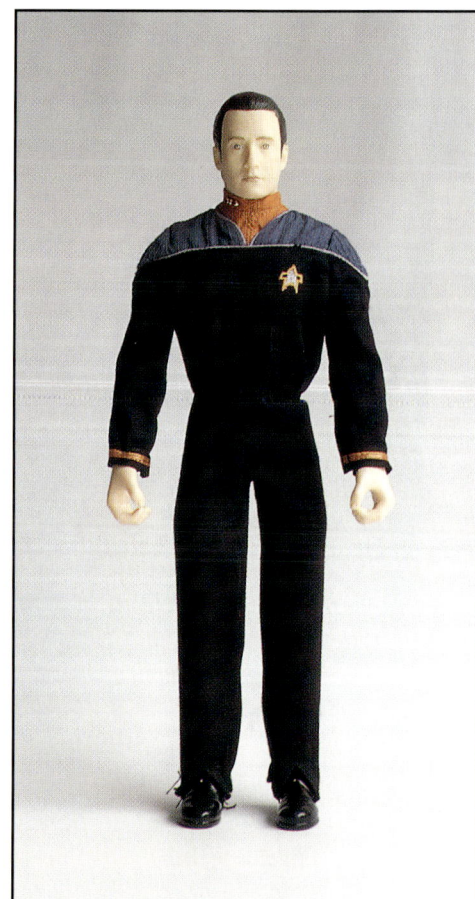

Assort. No. 65500 All *Star Trek* Series 1999

Mr. Spock
Stock No. 65501
Classic Edition – First in a Series
Phaser
Tricorder
Communicator
Vulcan Harp
Value: $30.00

Lt. Commander Geordi LaForge as seen in the film *Star Trek: Insurrection*
Stock No. 65504
Phaser rifle
Tricorder
Engineering tool
Value: $30.00

Captain Kathryn Janeway
Stock No. 65503
Women of Star Trek – First in a Series
PADD
Tricorder
Phaser
Value: $30.00

Andorian Ambassador Shras as seen in *TOS*
Stock No. 65051
Aliens and Adversaries Edition – First in a Series
Two beverage bottles
Two glasses
Value: $30.00

Assort. No. 65510 All *Star Trek* Series 1999

Seven of Nine as seen in *Voyager*
Stock No. 65512
Women of Star Trek Edition
Borg alcove
Phaser rifle
Value: $30.00

12" Seven of Nine
in packaging.

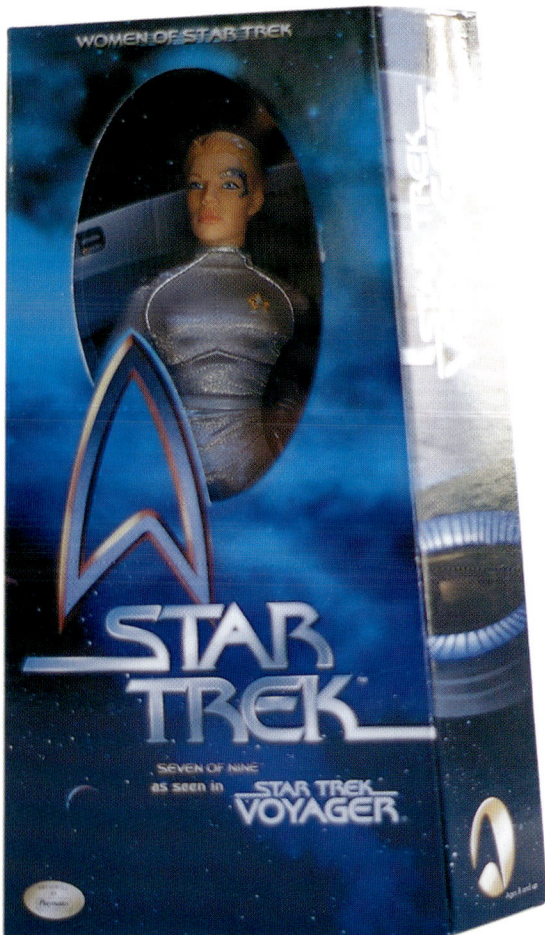

Doctor McCoy as seen in *TOS*
Stock No. 65521
Phaser
Tricorder
Communicator
Value: $30.00

Ensign Pavel Chekov
Stock No. 65531
Classic Edition
Tricorder
Phaser
Communicator
Value: $30.00

The Mugato as seen in *TOS*
Stock No. 65061
Aliens and Adversaries Edition
No accessories with the figure
Value: $30.00

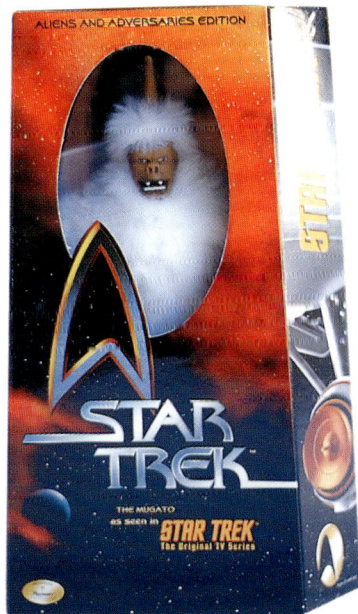

Assort. No. 65520 All *Star Trek* Series 1999

Counselor Deanna Troi
Stock No. 65511
Women of Star Trek
Tricorder
Phaser
PADD
Away team gear
Value: $30.00

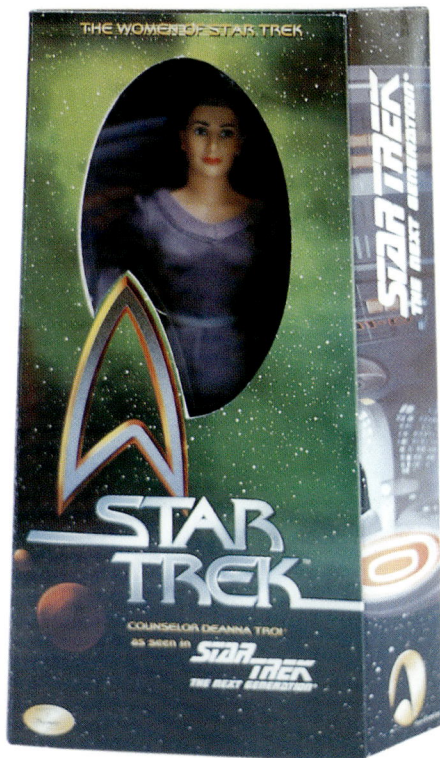

Chief Engineer Montgomery Scott
Stock No. 65522
Classic Edition
Phaser
Communicator
Engineering tools
Value: $30.00

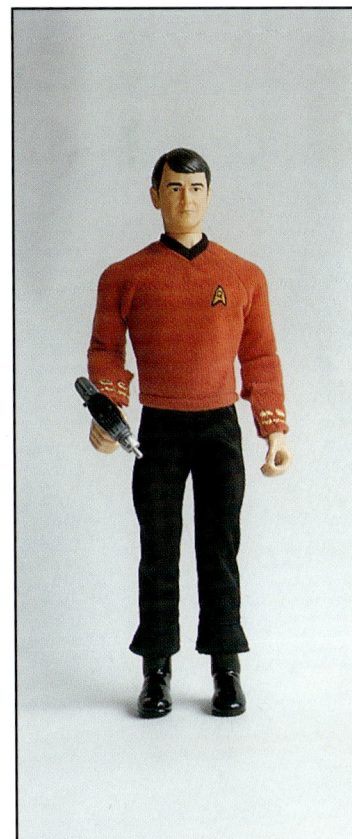

Lt. Hikaru Sulu
Stock No. 65523
Classic Edition
Tricorder
Phaser
Communicator
Value: $30.00

Gorn Captain as seen in *TOS*
Stock No. 65052
Aliens and Adversaries Edition
Staff
Stone Spike
Metron recorder/translator
Value: $30.00

Star Trek Communicator 12" Exclusive Figure

Captain Kirk as Romulan
Limited to only 3500. Comes with a certificate of authenticity but no accessories.
Value: $60.00

From the private collection of Dean Andrade. *Photo taken by Dean Andrade.*

Miniature Playsets and Figures

USS Enterprise NCC-1701-D Mini playset
Stock No. 6131
Innerspace Series 1995
Includes three 1" figures Captain Picard, Cmdr. Riker and

Lt. Cmdr. Data.
Also Included is a miniature shuttlecraft Goddard.
Ship opens up to reveal a mini bridge playset.
Value: $25.00

Assort. No. 6175 Innerspace Series 1995

Ferengi Marauder Mini Playset
Stock No. 6133
Includes two 1" figures, Picard and Ferengi
Mini clip out card on the packaging
Value: $8.00

Cardassian Galor-class Warship Mini Playset
Stock No. 6134
Includes two 1" figures, Odo and Gul Dukat
Mini clip out card on the packaging
Value: $8.00

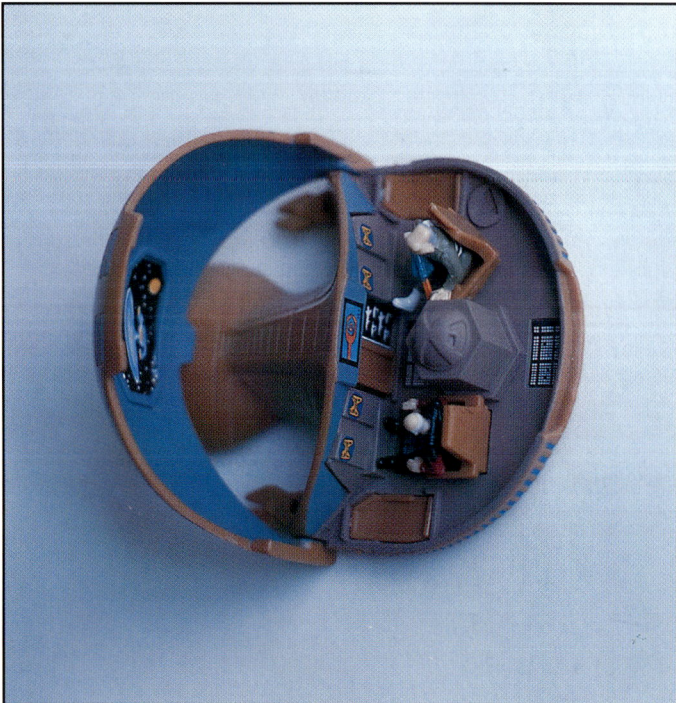

USS Stargazer Starship Mini Playset
Stock No. 6135
Includes two 1" figures, Picard and Q
Mini clip out card on the packaging.
Value: $8.00

Excelsior-class Starship Mini Playset
Stock No. 6137
Includes two 1" figures, LaForge and Riker
Mini clip out card on the packaging
Value: $8.00

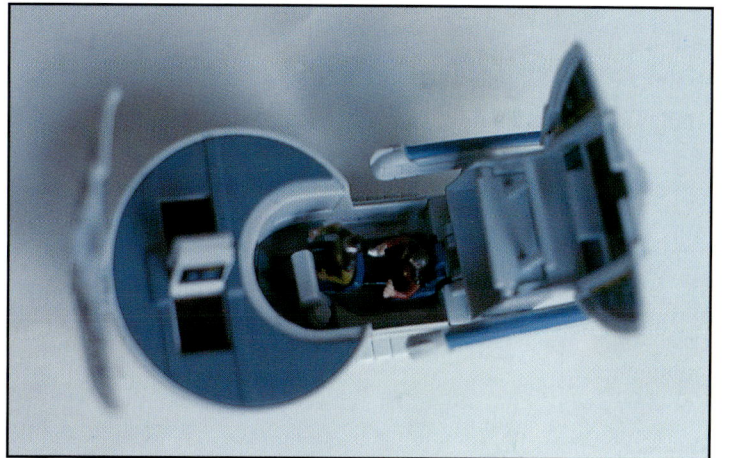

Galileo NCC-1701/7 Mini Playset
Stock No. 6139
Includes two 1" figures, Captain Kirk and Engineer Scott
Mini clip out card on the packaging
Value: $8.00

Apollo Lunar Excursion Module
Stock No. 6164
Includes two 1" NASA mini action figures
Mini clip out card on the packaging
Not truly *Star Trek*, but the packaging has the *Star Trek Innerspace* design.
Value: $8.00

Type II Phaser Mini Playset
Stock No. 6166
Includes three 1" figures, Lt. Cmdr. Worf, Q and Lt. Cmdr. Data
When closed the playset looks just like a Type II phaser.
Phaser opens to reveal an alien world playset.
Value: $10.00

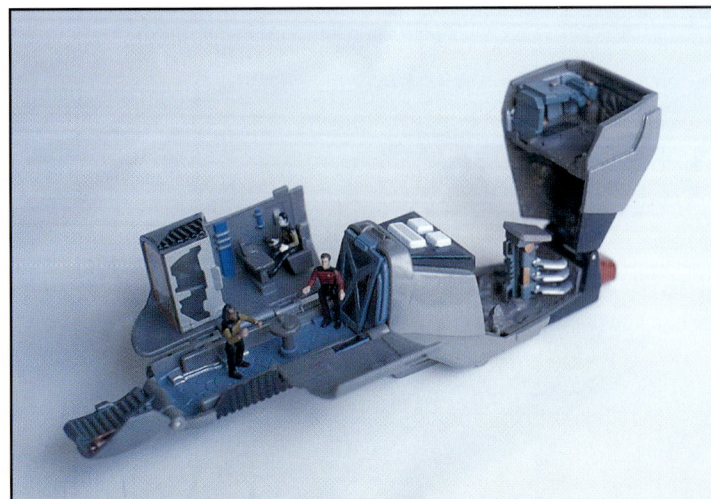

Medical Tricorder Mini Playset

Stock No. 6167

Includes three 1" figures, Dr. Crusher, Lt. Cmdr. LaForge and Picard as Locutus

Medical tricorder opens to reveal medical bay and bio lab playsets.

Value: $10.00

Communicator Mini Playset

Stock No. 6168

Includes two 1" figures, Cmdr. Riker and Lt. Cmdr. Data

Communicator opens to reveal transporter room with two "working" pads.

Value: $10.00

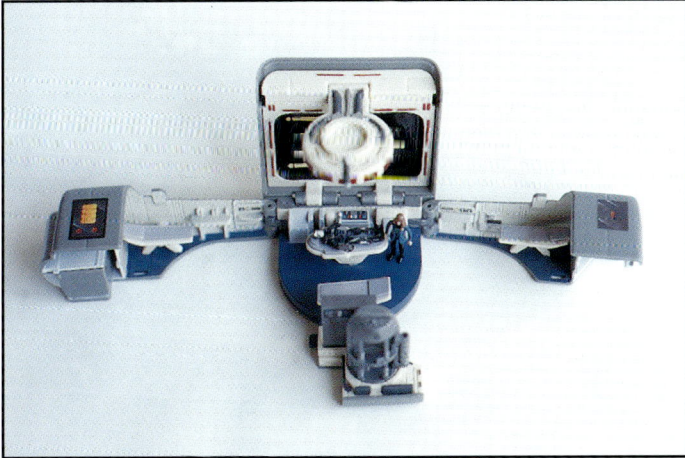

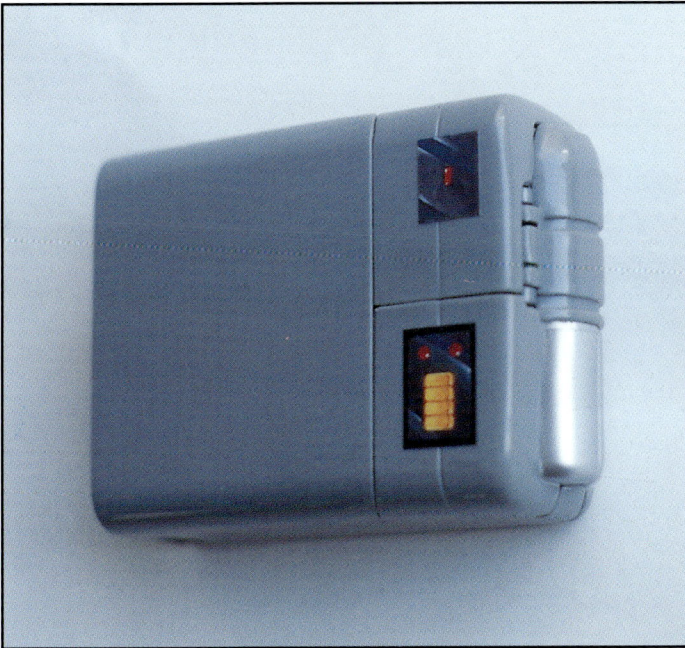

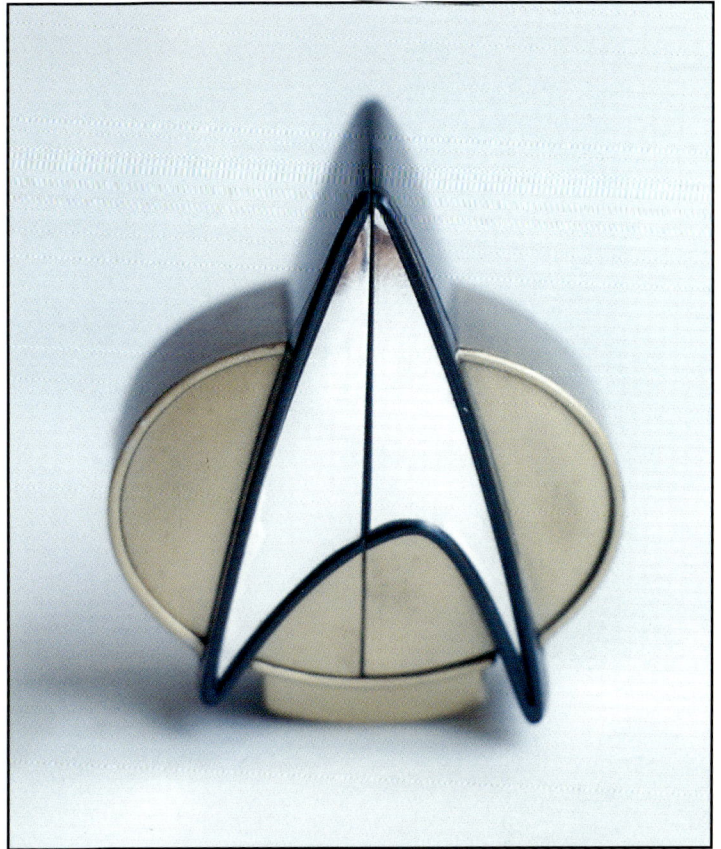

Apollo Command and Service Module
Stock No. 6169
Includes two 1" NASA mini action figures
Mini clip out card on the packaging
Not truly *Star Trek*, but the packaging has the *Star Trek Innerspace* design.
Value: $8.00

Shuttle Craft Goddard
Stock No. 6176
Includes two 1" figures, Lt. Cmdr. LaForge and Cmdr. Troi
Mini clip out card on the packaging
Value: $8.00

Borg Ship
Stock No. 6177
Includes two 1" figures, Borg drone and Picard
Mini clip out card on the packaging
Value: $8.00

Klingon Bird-of-Prey
Stock No. 6178
Includes two 1" figures, Lt. Cmdr. Worf and Gowron
Mini clip out card on the packaging
Value: $8.00

Romulan Warbird
Stock No. 6179
Includes two 1" figures, Sela and Picard as a Romulan
Mini clip out card on the packaging
Value: $8.00

USS Defiant Mini Playset
Stock No. 6180
Includes two 1" figures, Captain Sisko and Lt. Cmdr. Worf
   in DS9 uniform
Mini clip out card on the packaging
Value: $8.00

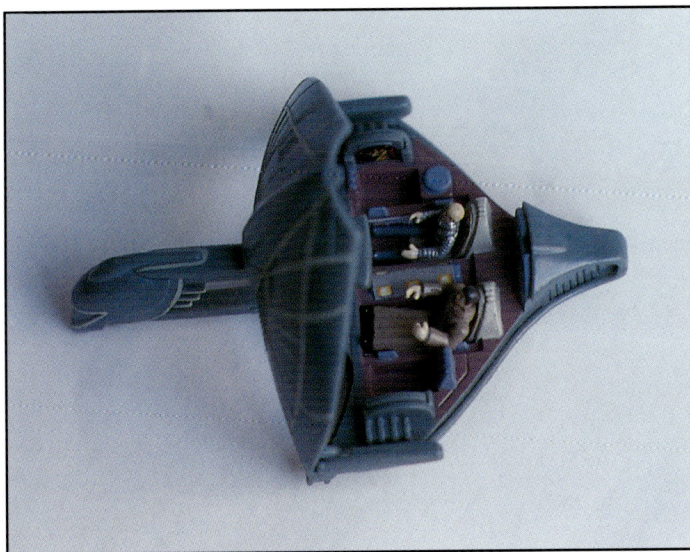

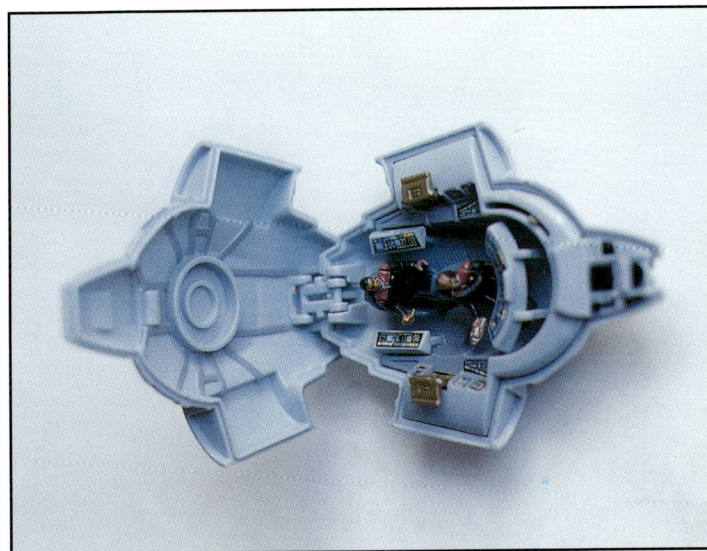

Assort. No. 16210 Strike Force Ships 1997

All ships come with a display stand and two unique figures.

Cardassian Warship
Stock No. 16211
Includes two 1" figures, Gul Dukat and Garak
Value: $10.00

USS Enterprise NCC-1701-D
Stock No. 16212
Includes two 1" figures, Captain Picard and Cmdr. Riker
Value: $10.00

Klingon Bird-of-Prey
Stock No. 16213
Includes two 1" figures, Valkris and Commander Kruge
Value: $10.00

Ferengi Marauder
Stock No. 16214
Includes two 1" figures, Daimon Bok and Jason Vigo
Value: $10.00

Maquis Fighter
Stock No. 16215
Includes two 1" figures, Chakotay and Torres in Maquis outfits
Value: $10.00

Assort. No. 16240 Strike Force Playsets 1997

Klingon Great Hall Playset
Stock No. 16241
Includes three 1" figures, Lt. Worf, K'Mpec Gowron, Klingon warrior and a targ
Klingon head opens to reveal great hall playset.
Value: $15.00

Borg Temple
Stock No. 16242
Includes four 1" figures, Lt. Cmdr. Data, Lore, Hugh Borg and a Borg soldier
Borg head opens to reveal miniature playset of the Borg temple as seen on *ST:TNG*.
Value: $15.00

Assort. No. 16270 Strike Force Figure Packs 1997

Each figure pack contained seven 1″ figures. The figures also fit in and work well with the strike force playsets and ships.

Klingon Warriors
Stock No. 16271
Lt. Worf in Klingon attire
Kahless
K'Ehleyr
Kurn
B'Etor
Two Klingon warriors
Value: $7.00

Starfleet Away Team
Stock No. 16272
Seven different Starfleet secu-
 rity personnel from *TNG,
DS9* and *Voyager*
Value: $7.00

Borg Assimilation Team
Stock No. 16273
Locutus
Borg Queen
Five different Borg soldiers
 from *TNG, Voyager* and *ST:
First Contact*
Value: $7.00

Ferengi Commerce Team
Stock No. 16274
Grand Nagus Zek
Letek
Rom
Brunt
Bel
Quark in Klingon attire
Nausicaan
Value: $7.00

Playsets For Use With 4.5" Figures

Bridge Set
Stock No. 6103
1993
Holds the entire bridge crew
Light-up view screen
Working bay doors
Eight sounds: view screen on, phaser, tractor beam, photon torpedo, hailing frequency, computer, warp drive, and red alert.
Technical blueprint
Value: $120.00

Transporter Room
Stock No. 6104
1993
Special transporting effects so figures *beam* in and out.
Authentic transporter sounds and light-up transporter chamber.
Bonus technical blueprints
Value: $40.00

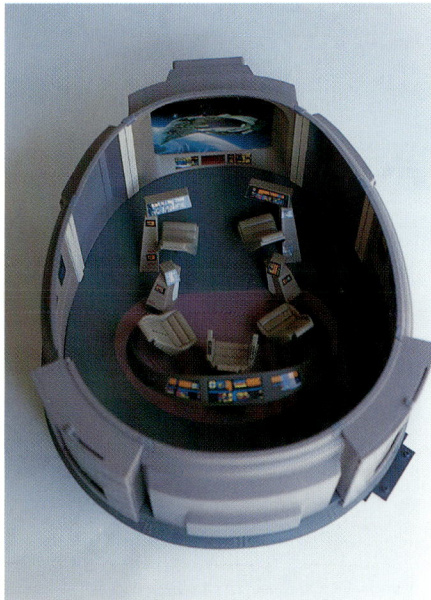

Bridge set viewed from the back.

Engineering Playset
Stock No. 6108
1994
Engineering stool and laser probe
Light-up warp core
Three sounds: power up, emergency warning and core breach explosion
Holds up to five 4.5" figures.
Value: $45.00

Bridge set with a full bridge crew.

Ships

Shuttle Craft Goddard
Stock No. 6101
1992
Light-up thrusters
Two different sounds phasers and impulse engines.
Holds three 4.5" crew members and has a removable
    cargo pallet.
Value: $35.00

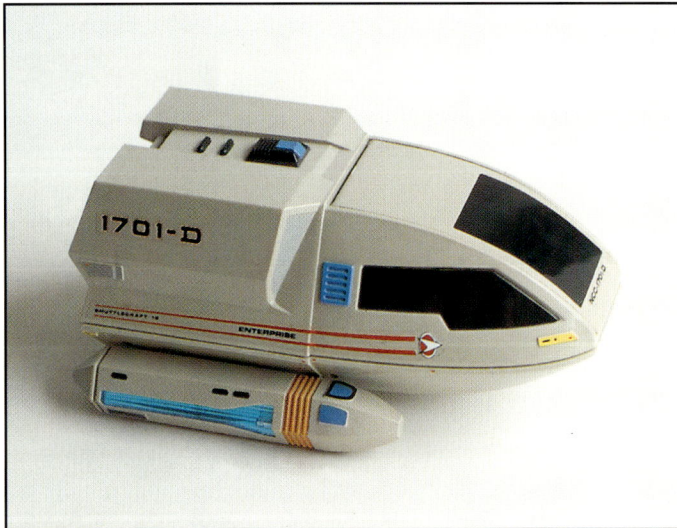

Starship Enterprise D
Stock No. 6102
1992
15" scale replica of the Enterprise D
Four different sounds: phaser, photon torpedo, impulse
    engines, and warp engines
Light-up warp nacelles
Bonus technical blue prints
Value: $40.00

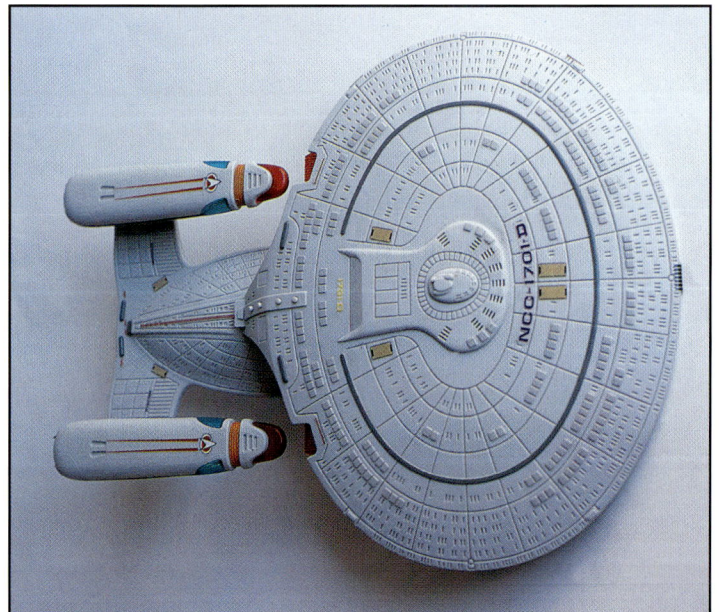

Gold Enterprise D
Stock No. 6112
1993
Gold painted 7th anniversary special collector's edition
    Starship Enterprise
Four sounds: warp drive, impulse engines, phasers, and
    photon torpedoes
Dual light-up engines
Display stand with numbered plaque
Certificate of authenticity
Limited production of 50,000 pieces
Value: $90.00

Enterprise D Glider
Stock No. 6113
1993
18" flying replica
Value: $20.00

Romulan Warbird
Stock No. 6154
1993
Light-up engines
Four sounds: cloaking, phaser, hit shields, and engines
Technical blueprints
Value: $40.00

Klingon Attack Cruiser
Stock No. 6155
1993
Light-up engines
Four sounds: cloaking, disruptor cannon, hit shields and
phaser
Bonus technical blue prints
Value: $40.00

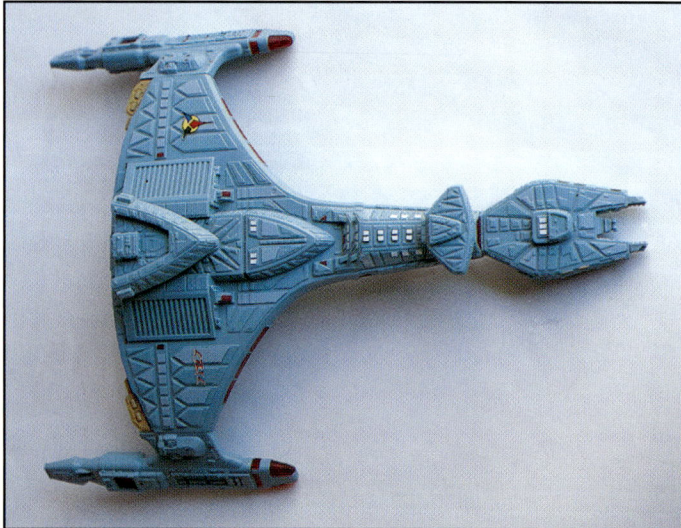

Space Station DS9
Stock No. 6251
1994
Light-up sail towers
Four sounds: tractor beam, photon torpedo, phaser and
docking
The station sits on a rotating display stand and comes
with a miniature Enterprise D to dock at DS9.
Bonus technical blueprints and certificate of authenticity
Value: $50.00

Borg Cube
Stock No. 6158
1994
Light-up interior
Three sounds: engines, tractor beam and laser cannon
Borg display stand
Certificate of authenticity
Value: $35.00

Runabout Orinoco
Stock No. 6252
1994
Light-up engine nacelles
Two sounds: phasers and opening wormhole
Technical blueprints
Certificate of authenticity
The runabout holds two 4.5" figures and has hinged front
and rear hatches.
Value: $30.00

Enterprise D with battle damage

Stock No. 6171
1994
Blow apart battle damage
Flashing lights and explosive sounds
Light-up engine nacelles
Three different sounds: photon torpedo, warning signal and explosion.
Bonus technical blueprints
Came in either the standard TNG packaging or in the Generation movie packaging.
Value: $40.00; TNG packaging: $120

Klingon Bird-of-Prey as seen in the film *Generations*

Stock No. 6174
1994
Light-up engine exhaust and torpedo launcher
Three sounds: torpedo, disruptor and engine cruise
Mini movie poster
Display stand
Technical blue prints
Value: $35.00; TNG packaging: $150.00

USS Enterprise NCC-1701-B as seen in the film *Generations*

Stock No. 6172
1994
Four different sounds from the movie: Nexus ribbon, phaser, tractor beam, and red alert
Mini Movie poster
Display stand
Value: $135.00

Space Talk Series USS Enterprise NCC-1701-D

Stock No. 6106
1995
First talking starship Enterprise.
Over 100 actual computer commands and sound effects from the TV show.
Display stand
Technical blueprints
Value: $30.00

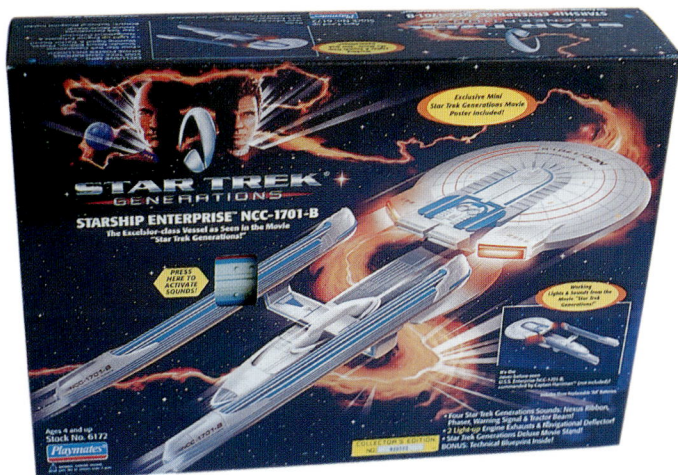

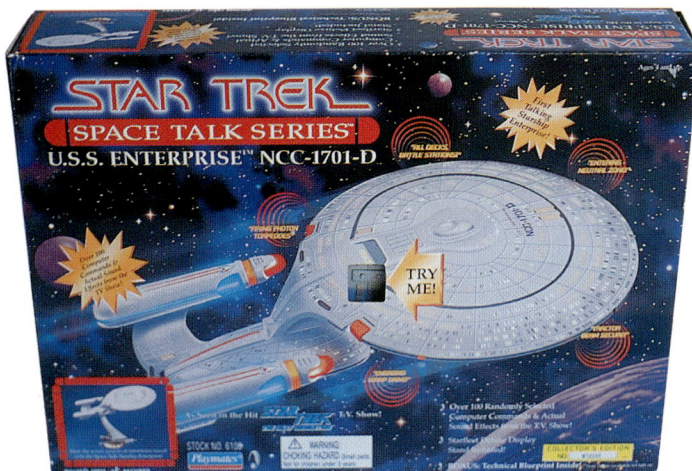

USS Enterprise NCC-1701

Stock No. 6116

1995

Four sounds: photon torpedoes, phasers, warp drive, and
    bridge interior

Light-up engine nacelles

Display stand

Value: $50.00

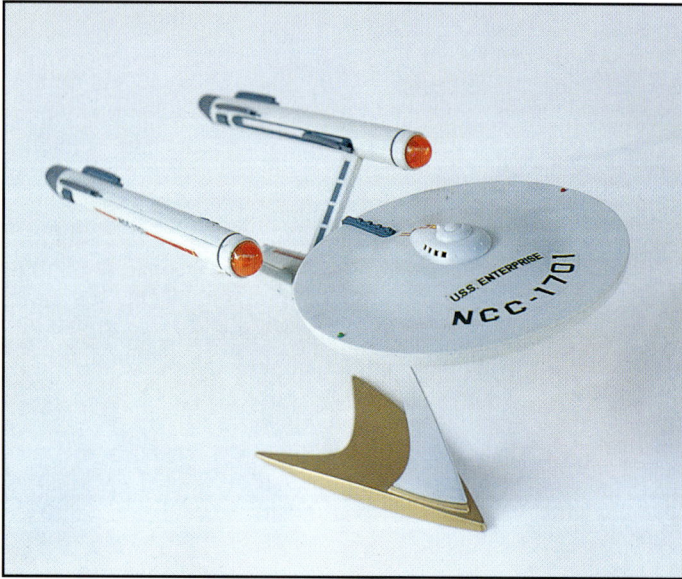

Starship USS Voyager from the television series *Star Trek: Voyager*

Stock No. 6479

1995

Light-up deflector

Automatic pivoting nacelles

Two sounds: photon torpedoes and warp speed

Display stand

Value: $125.00

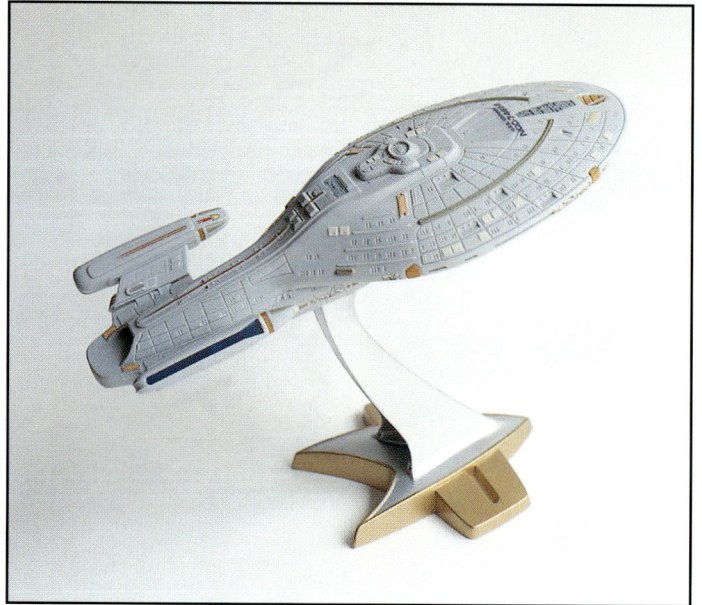

USS Excelsior NCC-2000

Stock No. 6127

1995

Four sounds: energy ribbon, phaser, warning signal, and
    tractor beam

Light-up engine exhausts and navigational deflector

Display base

Value: $120.00

Transwarping Enterprise

Stock No. 16077

1996

Two ships in one.

Transforms from Enterprise-D into the future Enterprise
    as seen in the episode *All Good Things*.

Display stand

Value: $40.00

Transwarping
Enterprise D

Warped into the
future vision of
the Enterprise.

Borg Sphere as seen in the film *Star Trek: First Contact*
Stock No.
Three different sounds
Pop off panel with light-up detailed battle damage
Display base
Value: $25.00

Phoenix Warp Drive Ship as seen in the film *Star Trek: First Contact*
Stock No. 16147
1996
Two button-activated sounds third is activated by pulling the thruster to deploy the pivoting nacelles.
Value: $30.00

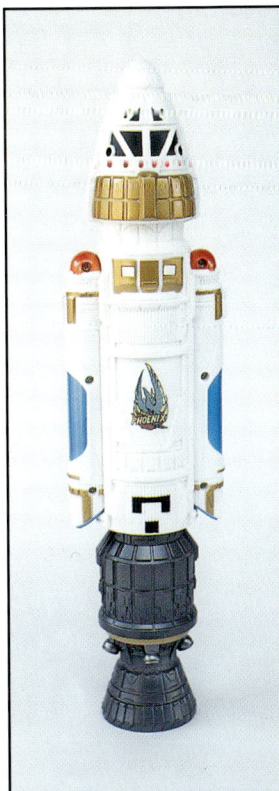

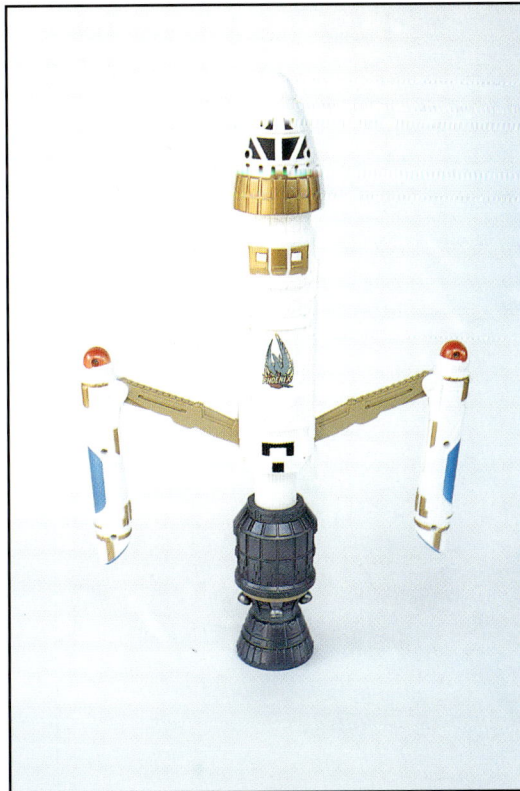

USS Enterprise NCC-1701-E as seen in the film *Star Trek: First Contact*
Stock No. 16148
1996
Light-up warp nacelles and impulse engines
Three sounds
Display base
Value: $40.00

Shuttle Craft Galileo with and exclusive Kirk figure as seen in the episode *From Where No Man has Gone Before*
Stock No. 16087
1996
Spring powered laser cannon
Value: $25.00

Romulan Bird-of-Prey as seen in *TOS*
Stock No. 16126
1997
Light-up engine nacelles
Four different sounds: phaser, photon torpedo, cloaking, and bridge interior
Romulan display stand
Value: $25.00

USS Defiant NX-74205 Valiant-class Prototype Destroyer as seen in *DS9*
Stock No. 16140
1997
Light-up engine nacelles
Four different sounds: cloaking device, photo torpedo, phaser, and red alert
Display stand
Value: $40.00

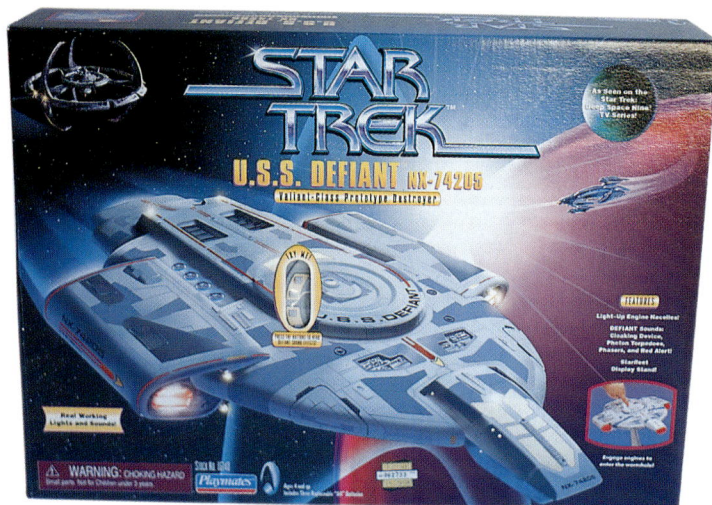

USS Enterprise NCC-1701-E as seen in the film *Star Trek: Insurrection*
Stock No. 65091
With Captain's Yacht
1998
Light-up warp nacelles and impulse engines
Three different sounds
Display stand
Value: $25.00

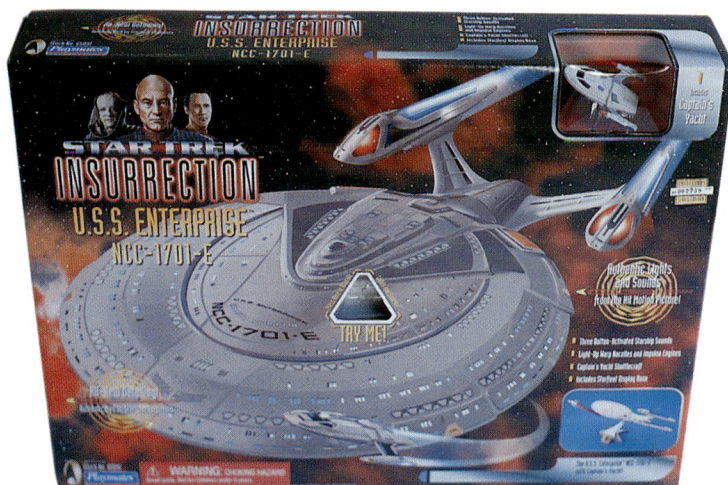

Role Playing Accessories

ST:TNG Phaser
Stock No. 6151
1992
Stun and disrupt sounds
Light-up phaser beam
Bonus technical blueprint
Value: $30.00

Personal communicator from *ST:TNG*
Stock No. 6152
1992
Communicator sound
Light-up insignia
Bonus technical blue prints
Communicator clips onto a shirt via a universal clip 'n
    plug backing on the communicator.
Value: $10.00

Tricorder as seen in *ST:TNG*
Stock No. 6153
1993
Light-up display screen and operating indicators
Three different sounds
Belt clip
Bonus technical blueprints
Value: $40.00

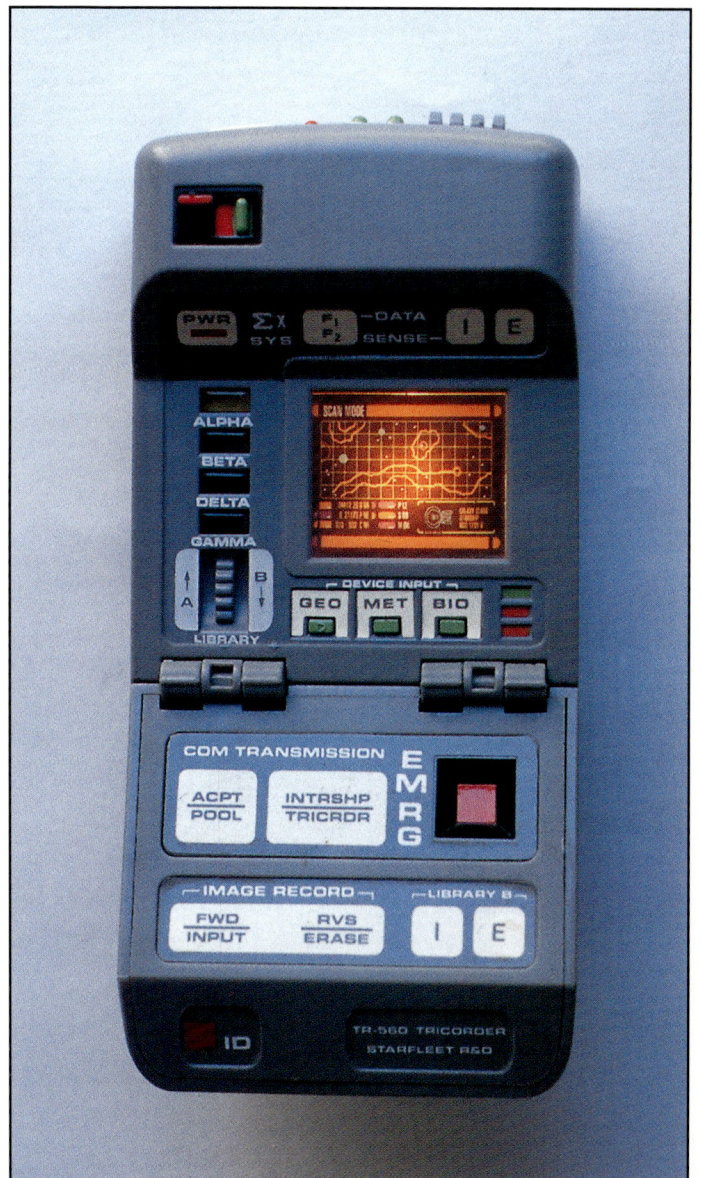

Communicator Walkie-Talkies

Stock No. 6119

1993

Communicator shaped walkie-talkies with a range of up to 150 feet.

Value: $25.00

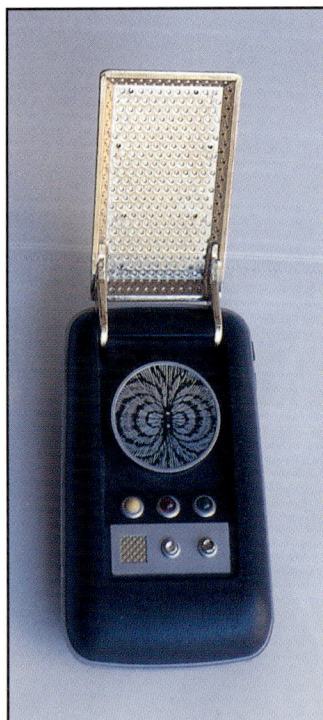

Classic Phaser

Stock No. 6118

1994

Light-up adjustable beam emitter

Two sounds: stun and higher setting

Certificate of authenticity

Technical blueprints

Value: $40.00

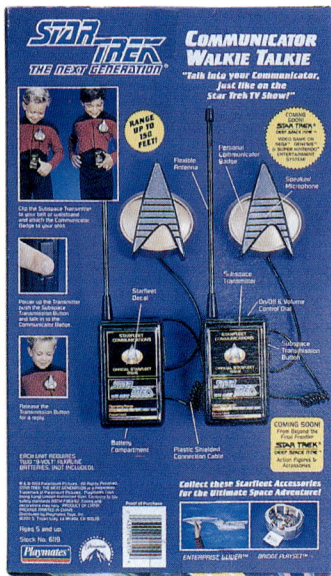

Classic Communicator

Stock No. 6117

1994

Three different sounds: opening, hailing and high frequency

Signal lights

Certificate of authenticity

Technical Blueprints

Value: $35.00

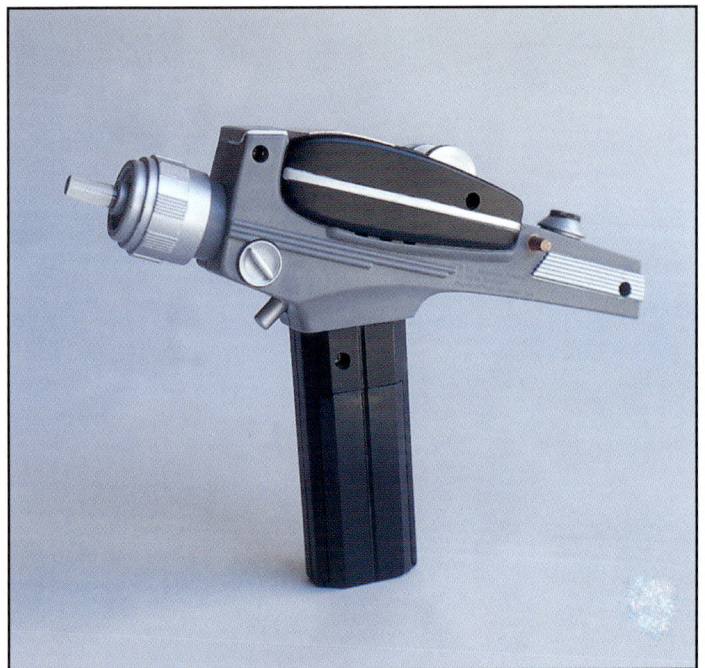

Classic Science Tricorder

Stock No. 6125

1995

Light-up view screen display

Flashing indicators

Scanning sounds

Shoulder strap

Bonus technical blueprints

Value: $30.00

Starfleet Communicator as seen in the film *Generations*
Stock No. 6147
1994
Light-up insignia
Communicator sound
Value: $10.00

Type I Phaser
Stock No. 6159
1994
Two phaser sounds: stun and disruption
Light-up phaser beam
Belt clip
Technical blueprints
Value: $30.00

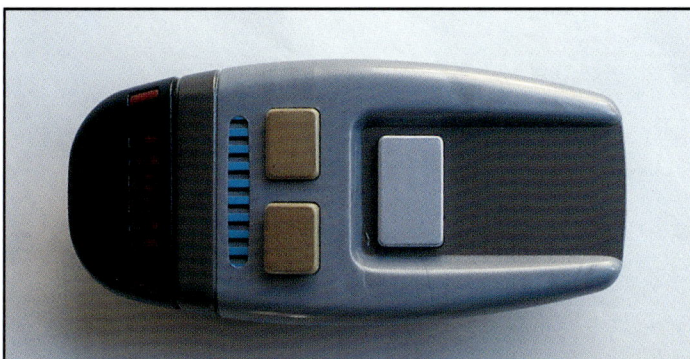

Klingon Disruptor
Stock No. 6129
1995
Light-up beam emitter
Two sounds: stun and disrupt
Technical blueprint
Value: $45.00; in Generations packaging: $25

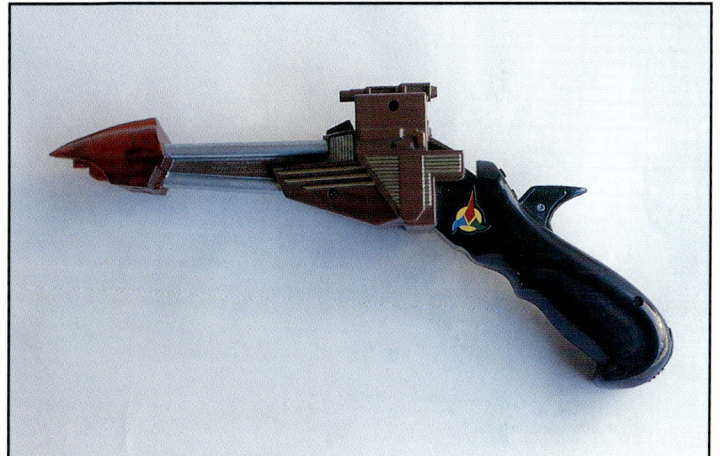

Bajoran Tricorder
Stock No. 6273
1995
Light-up view screen and flashing analysis indicators
Three different sounds
Value: $25.00

Bajoran Phaser
Stock No.
1995
Authentic lights and sounds
Value: $30.00

Talk-Back Classic Communicator
Stock No. 16065
1996
Working status light
Allows you to record up to a three-second message and
    play it back.
Starfleet communications guide
Value: $25.00

Starfleet Phaser as seen in the films *ST: TMP* and *Wrath of Khan*
Stock No. 16081
1996
Light-up energy beam emitter and power charge status
    indicators
Two phaser sounds
Belt clip
Value: $20.00

Starfleet Wrist Communicator as seen in the film *ST: TMP*
Stock No. 16082
1996
Light-up view screen and flashing indicators
Three sounds: hailing, comm scan and frequency control
Value: $15.00

Captain Pike's Laser Pistol as seen in the episode *The Cage*
Stock No. 16127
1997
Two sounds: stun and disrupt
Light-up beam emitter
Value: $15.00

Dr. McCoy's Medical Kit
Stock No. 16088
1996
Two piece set includes a medical scanner with digital scanning sound and an anabolic protoplaser with light-up laser tip.
Official Starfleet Medical School Diploma
Value: $25.00

Klingon D'K Tahg Knife
Stock No. 16142
1997
Two sound effects
Klingon knife sheath
Technical blueprint
Value: $15.00

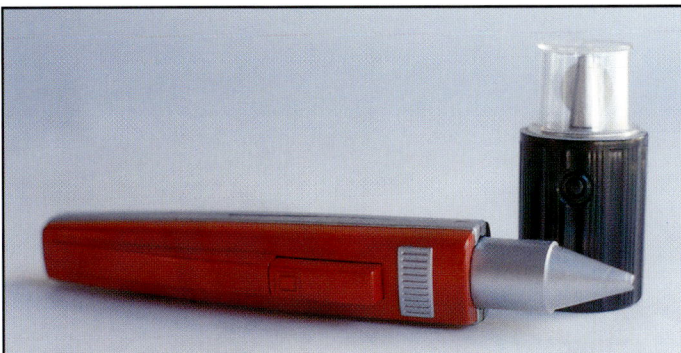

Medical Tricorder
Stock No. 16143
1997
Light up view screen and diagnostic indicators
Three different scanning sounds
Value: $20.00

Starfleet Phaser as seen in the film *ST:V The Undiscovered Country*
Stock No. 16144
1997
Light-up beam emitter
Two sounds: stun and disrupt
Removable battery clip
Technical blueprints
Value: $15.00

Starfleet Type II Phaser as seen in the film *Star Trek: Insurrection*
Stock No. 65088
Light-up power indicator and phased energy beam emitter
Two sounds: stun and disrupt
Belt clip
Value: $15.00

Resin Dioramas and Statues

Resin statues and dioramas were sculpted by the Steve Varner Studios. Each comes individually numbered and with a certificate of authenticity.

6" Resin Ultra Figures

Ultra Locutus
Stock No. 65001
Value: $60.00

Ultra Borg Queen
Stock No. 6500

12" Statues

Queen Borg
Stock No. 65021
Value: $100.00

Captain Picard
Stock No. 65022
Value: $100.00

*Photo courtesy of Jon
(Bart of Borg) Huss.*

Kirk from *Where No Man Has Gone Before*
Stock No. 65025
Value: $100.00

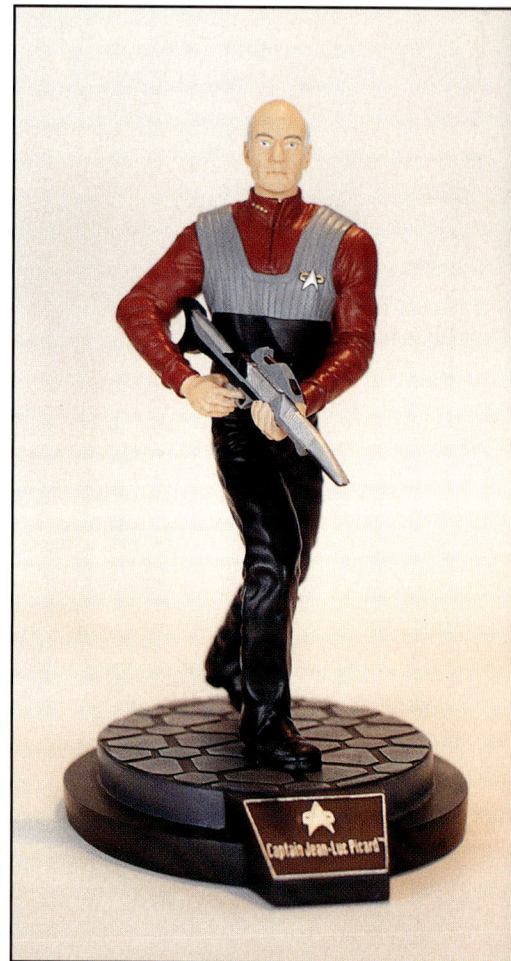

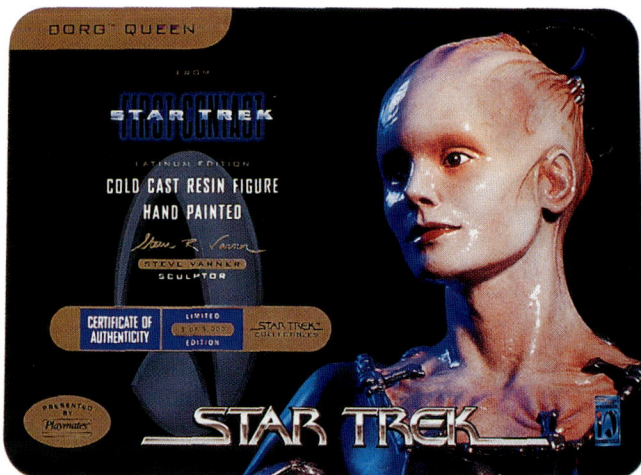

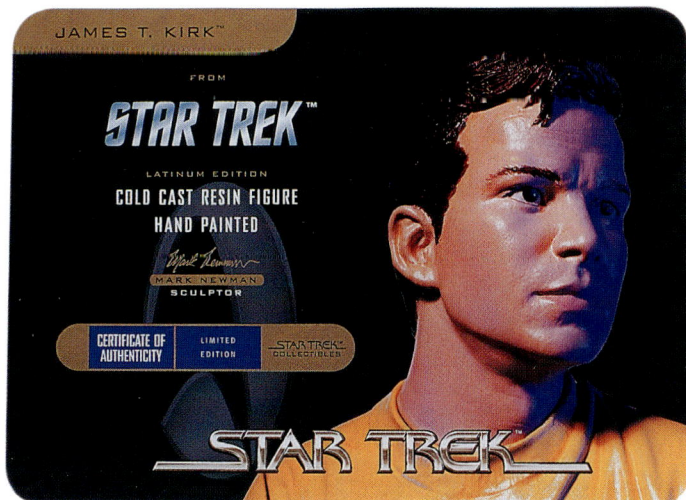

JAMES T. KIRK™

FROM

STAR TREK™

LATINUM EDITION
COLD CAST RESIN FIGURE
HAND PAINTED

MARK NEWMAN
SCULPTOR

CERTIFICATE OF AUTHENTICITY | LIMITED EDITION | STAR TREK COLLECTIBLES

STAR TREK™

Vulcan Leader from *First Contact*
Stock No. 65023
The Vulcan Leader was
never released in the
United States
Value: $300.00

From the private collection of
Andrew Novasitis. *Photo taken by
Andrew Novasitis.*

Seven of Nine
Stock No. 65026
Value: $100.00

Dioramas

Data and the Queen Borg in Engineering from *First Contact*
Stock No. 65030
Value: $100.00

*Photo courtesy of Jon
(Bart of Borg) Huss.*

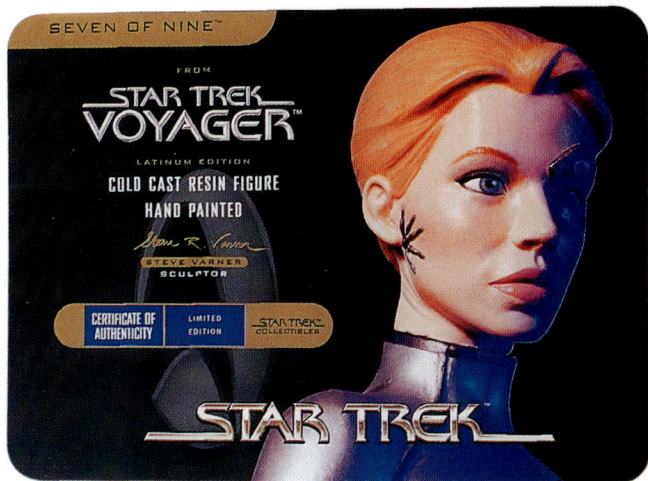

SEVEN OF NINE™

FROM

STAR TREK
VOYAGER™

LATINUM EDITION
COLD CAST RESIN FIGURE
HAND PAINTED

STEVE VARNER
SCULPTOR

CERTIFICATE OF AUTHENTICITY | LIMITED EDITION | STAR TREK COLLECTIBLES

STAR TREK™

Kirk and Spock from *Mirror, Mirror*
Stock No. 65032
Value: $50.00

From the private
collection of
Andrew Novasitis.
*Photo taken by
Andrew Novasitis.*

QVC Exclusive Ornament 1993

The Star Trek: The Next Generation Personal Communicator Ornament (stock no. 6162) was only available through the QVC home shopping network. The ornament is exactly the same as the personal communicator (stock no. 6152) that Playmates produced except it is made to hang on your holiday tree. The packaging was even very similar. 100,000 ornaments were made. *Value: $60.00*

Assort. No. 3450 Teenage Mutant Ninja Turtles 1994

Other than Star Trek, one of Playmates hottest toy lines was the Teenage Mutant Ninja Turtles. Playmates made a crossover line, having the Turtles appear as some of our favorite Trekkies. Each figure came with an exclusive Skybox trading card and a compliment of classic Trek accessories.

Captain Leonardo
Stock No. 3451
Communicator
Phaser
Tricorder
Katana
Star Trek shell base
Value: $15.00

Chief Engineer Michaelangelo
Stock No. 3452
Classic communicator
Phaser
Tricorder
Nunchakus
Star Trek shell base
Value: $15.00

Chief Medical Officer Raphael
Stock No. 3453
Communicator
Phaser
Tricorder
Sais
Star Trek shell base
Value: $15.00

First Officer Donatello
Stock No. 3454
Communicator
Phaser
Tricorder
Battle bo
Star Trek shell base
Value: $15.00

Signed Toys

The joy of collecting toys can be combined with the fun of autograph collecting. Here are a few figures that have been signed by the actors that played the characters portrayed by the toys. There is quite a bit of planning involved with getting toys signed; knowing who is going to be where and dragging the toys along to conventions to have them signed. Besides conventions, signed figures can be found on the internet and from dealers. Just be careful that you are getting the real thing. You can even get some signed figures directly from the actors. Majel sells hers on the web from her site .

The value of an autographed toy is basically the value of the toy plus the value of the signature. Some dealers consider a signed toy to be about three times the regular value of the figure.

Kes the Ocampa signed by
Jennifer Lein *Value: $60.00*

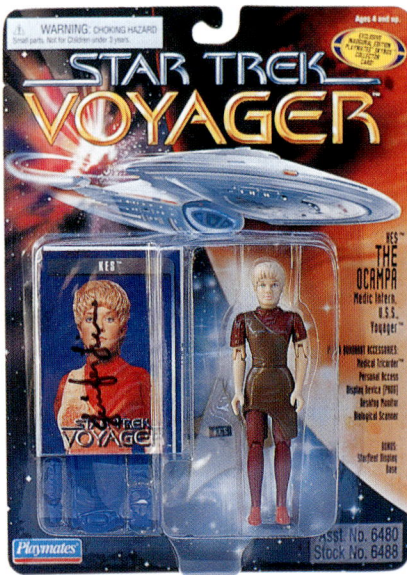

Odo signed by Rene Auberjonois
Value: $35.00

Quark signed by Armin
Shimerman *Value: $45.00*

Kira Nerys signed by
Nana Vistor
Value: $45.00

Gowron signed by
Robert O'Reilly
Value: $85.00

Appendix A

Skybox Trading Cards and Space Caps

Cards from the second series figures.

Cards from the Command Edition 9" figures.

Assorted space caps.

Cards from DS9 figures.

Space Caps from DS9 figures.

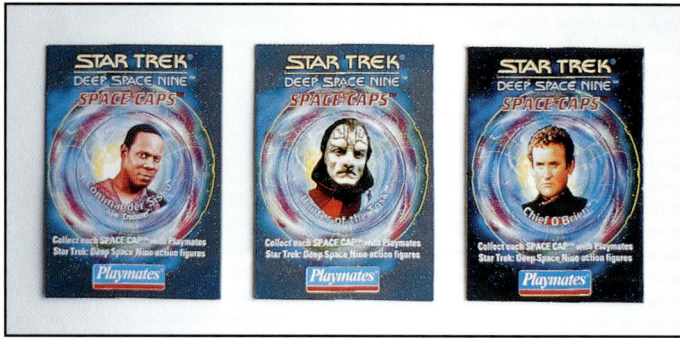

Cards from Voyager figures.

Card and pog variations.

Cards from 30th anniversary figures.

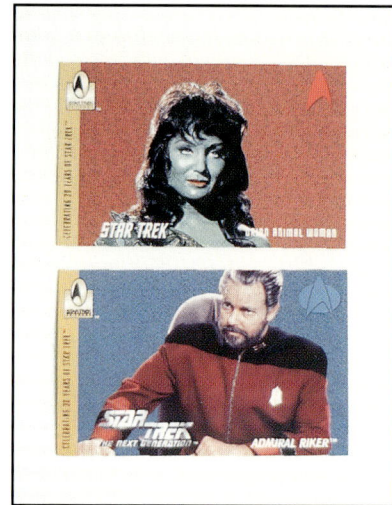

Cards from later series of figures are larger.

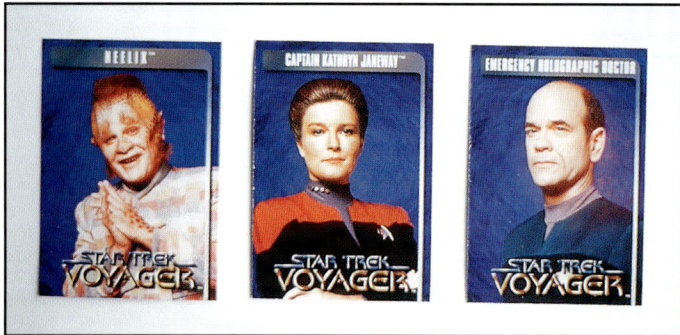

Cards from the classic movie figures.

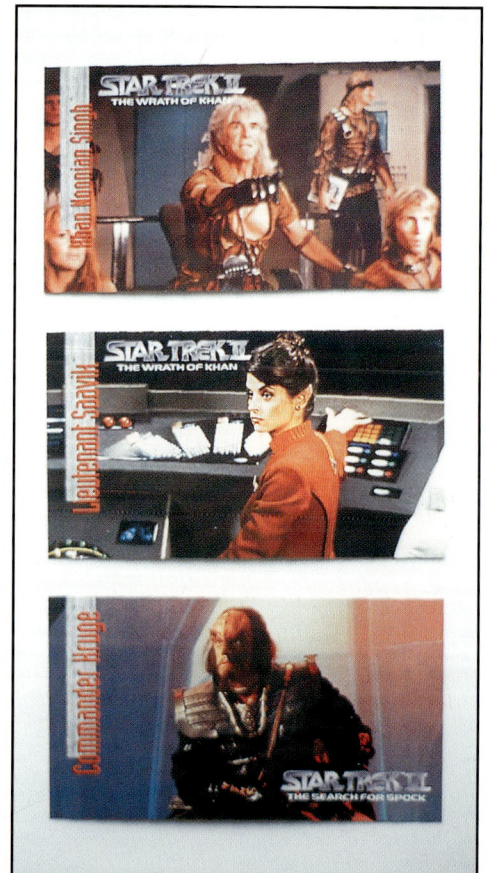

Appendix B

Non-Playmates Items

Soon after the first series of the 4.5" figures came out, a vinyl carrying case came out. Made by Tara Toy Corp. in 1993, this case can hold 12 figures and accessories. *Value: $5.00*

Playmates Protectors are plastic protective cases. The two-piece snap together cases are designed to protect your mint on card collection. *Retail: $2.00-5.00*

Appendix C

Finding Playmates...

Playmates Toys website:
http://www.playmatestoys.com/
To find out more about the different variations of each figure, check out Rene's website at:
http://members.aol.com/RDBousquet/StarTrk.html
Join in on the fun of collecting Playmates Toys with Playtrek, an online group gathered to discuss, trade and sell Playmates Star Trek toys via email. Find out more at:
http://playtrek.cjb.net/
To get the latest news and information about Trek toys and so much more, go to *Raving Toy Maniac* at:
http://www.toymania.com/news/startrek.shtml
Get your exclusives and hard to find Playmates figures from Rick at New Force Comics and Collectibles at:

New Force Comics and Collectibles
P.O. Box 1314
Lynn Haven, FL 32444
Phone: (850) 769-1745
Fax: (850) 914-2161
http://www.newforcecomics.com
Check out all the Star Trek and other sci-fi collectibles at 800-trekker.com.
800-TREKKER
PO Box 13131
Reading, PA 19612
Phone: 800-TREKKER
Fax: 800-FAX-TREK
http://www.800-trekker.com
Organize your collection by using the online checklist at:
http://www.toymania.com/news/startrek/playlist/index.shtml
Pagaoda Comics has Playmates, Mego and Galoob Star Trek toys and much more.
Pagoda Comics
2966 St. Lawrence Ave
Reading, PA 19606
610-779-0664
http://www2.epix.net/~pagoda
Author's website:
http://members.aol.com/Playtrekbook/
Email: Playtrekbook@aol.com